CREATING WOODEN VILLAGES

CREATING WOODEN VILLAGES

Designs for 18 Miniature Buildings

Evan J. Kern

Color Renditions by Sarah Kern Grant

STACKPOLE
BOOKS

Published by
STACKPOLE BOOKS
5067 Ritter Road
Mechanicsburg, PA 17055

Printed in the United States of America

10 9 8 7 6 5 4 3 2 1

FIRST EDITION

Cover design by Caroline Stover

Library of Congress Cataloging-in-Publication Data

Kern, Evan J.
    Creating wooden villages : designs for 18 miniature buildings / Evan J. Kern : color renditions by Sarah Kern Grant.—1st ed.
        p.   cm.
    Includes bibliographical references.
    ISBN 0-8117-2782-3
    1. Miniature craft—United States. 2. Woodwork—United States—Patterns. 3. Historic buildings in art. 4. Cities and towns in art. 5. Jig saws. I. Title.
TT178.K46   1997
720'.22'8—dc21   97-19452
                                                                                            CIP

To Lucy and Sarah

CONTENTS

INTRODUCTION

The cities, towns, villages, and countryside of the United States abound with architectural treasures. On almost any road we take, any street we follow, wonderful buildings of various styles, constructed from a wide range of materials, will turn up. For example, on the block where I live in a small town in southeastern Pennsylvania, you can find a Pennsylvania German stone farmhouse, a two-story log building that was originally a store, houses in the Queen Anne style, Italianate houses, houses with mansard roofs, and structures of almost every architectural style from the eighteenth and nineteenth centuries. There's even a Cape Cod house from the middle of the twentieth century and, interestingly enough, an outhouse. These treasures deserve to be preserved, not only in photographs and architectural monographs, but also in the form of miniature wooden buildings—small replicas that show the details and nuances of their design and construction.

The making of miniature architectural replicas has a lengthy history. In the tomb of King Tut (Tutankhamen), built after his death in 1325 B.C., was found a stone replica of a shrine, complete with columns and statuary. In sixteenth-century Germany, some clocks were housed in metal replicas of cathedrals, the movement of the clock replacing the circular rose window of the cathedral. The nineteenth century saw the development of miniature dollhouses. And with the invention of mechanical toy trains later in that century came whole miniature towns to provide landscapes through which the toy trains could travel.

Today, we can find miniature wooden buildings—designed for display on mantels, windowsills, and shelves—in most craft shops and home decorating stores. They come in two varieties: "in-the-round," which shows all four sides of a building, and "flat," which is an outline of a building with a colored picture of its features either printed on or glued to the front. It is this latter type of miniature wooden buildings that you will learn to make.

I will take you step by step through the techniques. When you have finished the projects, you should be able to make miniature replicas of actual buildings in your community as well as buildings of your own design. I also hope that the information given on each building's history, style, and form of construction will help you understand the historic architecture of the United States—especially that of the mid-Atlantic states—and guide you in preserving some of the architectural treasures in your community.

You will find drawings here for over twenty buildings. I have seen and photographed each, choosing them from among hundreds of candidates. I used two criteria for my selections. First, each building had to have been built before 1900 in order to reflect the quality of life in American small towns and villages during the pastoral days. The second criterion was that each building had to be aesthetically pleasing.

The plan of the book is straightforward. The first chapter, Getting Started, introduces you to the basic processes, techniques, and materials used to make miniature wooden buildings. The second chapter takes you through each of the steps involved in making a miniature replica of the Kutztown Depot, a nineteenth-century Victorian railroad station. This chapter is followed with separate chapters for eighteen other buildings, each selected to help you acquire additional skills. In each chapter you will find information about a specific building—its location, date of construction, and style as well as notes about the historical significance it may have. This information is followed by drawings and instructions for making the building. The book concludes with a chapter on translating your own photographs of buildings into miniature wooden buildings.

1
GETTING STARTED

Making miniature wooden buildings requires certain materials and tools beyond the common tools usually found in a woodworker's or craftsman's shop. In this chapter I will recommend the ones that have worked best for me. To understand the choices, however, you need an overview.

CONSTRUCTION PROCESS

First, a photocopy is made of the drawing. Color and texture are then applied to the photocopy with colored pencils, and the colored drawing of the building is protected with fixative. Next, a piece of wood is cut to an appropriate size, and the colored picture is glued to the wood with a spray adhesive. Excess paper is trimmed from the edges of the wood. Then the building is cut out with a scroll saw, the edges are sanded and sealed, and a matching paint is applied to the edges and to the back of the building. The final step is to sign and date the building on the back.

When I began to make these miniatures, I assumed that I would simply trace a building's drawing onto a block of wood, cut it out, and then use paint to create the color, texture, and details of the building. I knew that mass production of the miniatures used methods such as silk screen and color lithography. However, I assumed that these commercial varieties had been inspired by meticulously hand-painted originals. Now I think I was wrong. It's simply too difficult to hand-paint the detail.

I tried first to trace the drawing onto the surface of the wood using carbon paper and a sharp pencil, but no matter how carefully I traced or how sharp the pencil was, I was unable to get the lines fine enough. Next I gave the piece of wood several coats of gesso (a white, plaster-like coating), thinking that with a better surface I could obtain a sharper tracing. I even tried tracing paper specially developed for craft use, again without much success. It then occurred to me to glue the paper drawing to the wood, cut out the building, and then paint it. I had no problems gluing the drawing to a block of wood or cutting out the building. So at least now I had the drawing on the wood and the wood in the shape of the building. I decided to paint it with acrylics. I quickly discovered, though, that I was unable to find any method of applying the paint that would achieve the details and textures I sought. I tried watercolors and colored markers only to fail again. I simply could not control any of the media with sufficient accuracy to achieve the details needed to give the buildings their unique character. (I did not try oil paints because earlier experiences with this medium suggested that it, too, would be beyond my control.) This was a very discouraging and unexpected discovery.

Some of my friends had small, hand-painted models of buildings, which I examined with interest. In each instance, the painting of the buildings was quite coarse and lacked that fine detail I was seeking. Even large objects like doors and windows were simply suggested with blobs and streaks of paint. I now realized that the craftsmen had never *tried* to achieve the degree of detail I thought necessary.

COLORED PENCILS

I was about ready to abandon the whole project when I discovered the ideal solution—colored pencils. They were easily controlled, capable of the smallest detail, and could produce almost any desired color or texture. They also are relatively inexpensive.

The only negative aspect of using colored pencils is a prejudice against them. I kept trying to find a substitute for the word "coloring" because I associated this word with children's coloring books and crayon drawings. I tried the

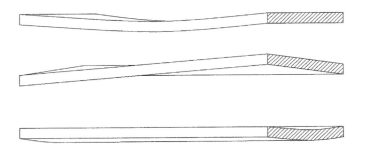

Lumber defects. Top, *warp is a bending of a board from end to end.* Center, *wind is a twisting of a board from edge to edge.* Bottom, *cup is the curvature of a board across its width.*

term "rendering," but that sometimes sounded awkward. Lacking a good alternative, I decided the word "coloring" was perfectly respectable and the best one to use in describing the process of adding color, texture, and details. So "coloring" it is, even if I am a bit uneasy with the term.

The material in colored pencils is a relatively hard, nonfluid substance usually applied in short, linear strokes, quite unlike the application of such fluid media as paints, inks, and markers. The colors can't be mixed together, as fluid media can, to attain a specific tone. Rather, the desired color or tone is achieved by the gradual application of one layer of color on top of another. The process requires a light touch and patience, but the rewards are great as you see an almost magical transformation of the black-and-white drawing into a colorful rendering of the building.

To assist you in the coloring, instructions with each building specify the color of the pencils and the techniques used for the different parts of the building. In the back of the book you will find a listing of all of the different colors and brands of pencils used. I would suggest, though, that you purchase a small starter set plus any additional pencils needed for the first two or three buildings. In this way you can test the techniques while minimizing your investment.

You will want to apply fixative to the drawings after you have colored them. This helps to ensure that the pigments from the colored pencils will not rub off. I use Krylon's Matte Finish No. 1311.

Once the fixative has dried, the colored picture is glued to a block of wood of an appropriate size with a spray adhesive. I use 3M's Super 77 Spray Adhesive, but there are many other adhesives on the market that probably work as well. A word of caution: Spray adhesives use solvents and aerosol gases that can be hazardous to your health. They should not be used without adequate ventilation.

WOOD BLOCK

All of the buildings presented in the book are intended to be made from ¾-inch-thick pine or a similar softwood. Many commercially produced wooden buildings use a material called medium density fiberboard, or MDF. It is less expensive than wood and free of defects, yet I find it wears out saw blades faster and can't be cut into the fine detail needed. Select wood that is as free of knots as possible, since the resins in knots, particularly in woods such as pine, have a tendency over time to bleed through layers of paper or paint and appear as brown stains on the surface. However, the board itself doesn't have to be knot-free as long as there are sufficient knot-free areas within it from which to cut the wood blocks needed for the buildings. I use a grade of wood known as select white pine. It has few knots and usually is straight—that is, free from *warp, wind,* or *cup.* Warp is the twisting of the board from end to end, wind is the twisting of a board from edge to edge somewhat like an airplane propeller, and cup is the curvature of the board across its width. You can check for these conditions when you are buying a piece of lumber simply by sighting down the length of the board and across the end to detect any deviation from straight, either sideways or up and down, or any curvature crosswise.

The drawings of buildings in this book are printed full size, and none require a block of wood larger than 6 inches in width and 8 inches in length. Therefore, a board 8 inches wide will accommodate all the drawings. Of course, an 8-inch board is not really that wide; that is a nominal dimension used for lumber that has been planed. The ones I purchase usually measure only 7¼ inches in width but are still wide enough for the purpose. The board can be of any convenient length. Lumber is sold in multiples of 2 feet and usually a minimum length of 8 feet. However, some lumber companies will cut you a piece shorter than this. Be sure the board you purchase has been jointed on both long edges and planed to thickness. In the trade this is known as "S4S"—surfaced four sides. This will provide a board with two smooth sides and edges that are square to the sides of the board.

Using a Scroll Saw

A scroll saw (also known as a jigsaw) is used to cut the outline of the buildings. Though a handsaw, such as a coping saw, could be used, its blades have large teeth and will tear fibers of wood on the back of the wood block. Additionally, it is very difficult to cut details that are fine enough for many of the buildings.

If you do not have access to a scroll saw and must rely upon a handsaw, then you should use a fretsaw. A fretsaw is similar to a coping saw but can use the same blades as those used with a scroll saw for cutting fine details. Its disadvantage lies in the time it takes to develop skill in following the outline of a building while simultaneously maintaining a vertical cut through the wood. If you choose to use a fretsaw, you will need a bench pin or "bird's beak" to support the wood while you are cutting it. The construction of a bench pin and the technique for cutting with a fretsaw are explained in my book *Making Wooden Jigsaw Puzzles* (Stackpole, 1996).

If you don't have a scroll saw and decide to purchase one, buy the best you can afford. A comprehensive discussion of the design and construction of scroll saws will be found in the same book. You also should consult woodworking magazines such as *Fine Woodworking* for articles comparing various brands and sizes of scroll saws. If at all possible, try using the saw before you purchase it so that you will have some insight into whether it will do the cutting task you have in mind. I use a Hegner 18-inch variable-speed saw. The variable speed is an especially valuable feature, as it allows me to select the best speed for cutting any particular material or for any specific saw blade.

The size and style of blades you use will in large measure determine the quality of the cut you make. For ¾-inch pine I use a PG07 ground, skip-tooth blade. The blade features widely spaced, precision-ground teeth. The teeth are extremely sharp and make very smooth-cut edges, and the large spaces between the teeth provide efficient sawdust removal. In addition, the lower teeth are reversed to reduce the tear-out common with conventional scroll saw blades.

Follow the instructions that came with your saw for installing blades. The tension on the blade should be as high as possible without breaking the blade or applying undue strain on the arms of your scroll saw. This will help ensure that the blade does not wander from side to side when you are cutting the outline of a building. You also will want to be sure that the saw blade is square with the saw table. If you use a saw that is out of square when you are cutting small details such as inside corners, you will find that the two saw cuts needed to make such a corner may not meet on one side or the other of the wood. Thus, the piece of waste wood will not come free without sawing past the intersection of the two lines.

An easy way to check whether the saw blade is square to the saw table is to place a small square on the saw table and move it until it just touches the blade. You may need to move the hold-down out of the way to do this. If the blade is exactly parallel to the edge of the square, then it also is square to the top of the saw table. If you do not have a square that is small enough to fit between the saw table and the upper blade clamp, you can make your own squaring tool. Joint a short piece of wood so that one edge is square to the sides. Rip the piece of wood so that it is just wide enough to fit between the scroll saw table and the upper blade clamp, or the hold-down at its highest position. Measure the width of the saw table and cut the board to this length. Measure the distance from the left edge of the saw table to the saw blade and make a pencil mark on the piece of wood the same distance from its left end. With a try square and a sharp pencil, draw a line the width of the board through the mark just made. Place the piece of wood directly behind the blade of the saw. The saw blade and the vertical mark on the board should be parallel to one another. If they aren't, adjust the angle of the table until they are. I actually prefer using this squaring device, because it stands unsupported on the saw table. Drill a small hole in one end and you can hang it on a nail handy to the scroll saw.

If you have not used a scroll saw before, you will soon discover that it is a great tool for cutting curved lines but not so great when cutting straight lines. This is because errors in cutting a straight line will appear much more obvious than errors in cutting a curved line. Unfortunately, miniature wooden buildings are made up almost entirely of straight lines—straight lines that intersect other straight lines forming inside corners and other shapes that cannot be cut on a machine designed specifically for cutting straight lines. The solution, of course, is to practice. Eventually you will learn to control the piece of wood so that cutting straight lines will no longer be a major problem.

Finally, you need to be aware that different brands and styles of scroll saw blades do not all cut in the same way. You would think, for example, that when you are cutting a straight line you would feed the wood squarely into the blade. However, you will soon discover that the blade has a mind of its own and will wander away from the line you are trying to cut. Over a period of time you may note that the blade almost always wanders off to the same side of the line. This is a fault of the blade (rarely the scroll saw), and you will have to learn to compensate for it by feeding the wood at a slight angle to the blade. Eventually, you will learn to cut all straight lines at this angle. You also can try a number of different makes of saw blades and then decide which blade works best for you. Remember, too, that a dull saw blade will not track properly. I always change blades when I begin cutting out a new building.

Painting the Wood

The raw edges of the wood are sealed before they are painted. Do not use a shellac sealer on the wood because it will prevent the paint from drying completely. I use Pactra's No. 71-4 Sanding Sealer, which both fills and seals the pores in the wood so that the paint will flow on more smoothly. I use Pactra's No. 43-4 to clean my brushes. Both are available at most hobby shops that sell wooden model airplane kits.

I use a basic set of liquid acrylic paints manufactured by Liquitex to mix the color needed for painting the edges and backs of the miniature buildings. The colors in my set are oxide red, raw umber, burnt umber, burnt sienna, phthalocyanine green, cadmium yellow, titanium white, mars black, ultramarine blue, and scarlet red. In the instructions in later chapters I will refer to the first four colors by their full names; the others I will call green, yellow, white, black, blue, and red.

Adding a few drops of Acrylic Flow Improver to the paint makes it easier to brush on smoothly. I suspect it is simply a detergent that acts by cutting down the surface tension. The flow improver I use is marketed by Winsor and Newton.

Finally, since my penmanship leaves much to be desired, I use a transparent, plastic label on the back of each miniature building to provide information about the building. I use Avery's Clear Laser Labels No. 2662, which are designed to be printed using a computer. Unfortunately, they can be used only with a laser printer.

The other tools and materials you will need, such as pencils, rulers, carbon paper, sandpaper, and drafting tape, usually can be found around the house or can be purchased without difficulty.

Now that you have explored the basic materials and tools, you can to begin your first project: a Victorian railroad station. I hope you find it both challenging and rewarding.

2

VICTORIAN RAILROAD STATION

In this chapter you will learn the basic processes and techniques used to make a miniature wooden building. You also will learn terminology architects and historians use when talking about the style and structure of buildings, and you will learn something about the history of the Victorian railroad station known locally as the Kutztown Depot.

The Kutztown Depot has a rural charm typical of hundreds of similar railroad stations in small towns and villages throughout the nation. This, plus the fact that it is of relatively simple construction, led me to choose it for your first project. Neither the coloring nor the cutting of the building should present any major problems. I think you will find it a good introduction to the craft.

The railroad station is located in Kutztown, a small town in southeastern Pennsylvania. Construction of the station began in 1869 and was completed the following year. Its style of architecture is known as Gothic Revival, a style that was popular in the United States between 1835 and 1880. It represents a return to building styles of the Middle Ages in Europe, combining French, Italian, and English elements with a free use of color. In the United States it also may be called American Gothic or Carpenter Gothic, the latter because of the extensive use of wood in the construction of American buildings in contrast to the use of stone and brick masonry in the earlier Gothic buildings of Europe. Since the station was built during the reign of Queen Victoria of England (1837–1901), it also can be called Victorian Gothic or simply Victorian, as I have done in the title of this chapter.

The Gothic features are the semiarches under the eaves, the scalloped lower edges of the roof rafters and crossbeam, and the framing of the windows and doors. The semiarches on either side of the building hide and protect the bracings used to support the extended eaves of the building. These eaves, in turn, protect the passengers and freight from the weather when entering the station from one side and boarding the train on the other side. The framing of the windows and doors are subtle imitations of the stonework surrounding the windows and doors in original Gothic buildings. The scallops on the bottom edges of the roof beams and the crossbeam are purely decorative elements.

The batten strip siding resulted from using a "post and beam" type of framing with the vertical corner posts placed on wood sills and connected to one another with heavy crossbeams. This form of construction was commonly used in the mid-Atlantic region for framing houses, barns, and other buildings during the eighteenth and nineteenth centuries. Boards were nailed between the sill and crossbeam and also between the crossbeam and roof beams. The gaps between the boards were then covered with battens. They helped keep out wind and rain. The batten strips used on the depot are unique in that they are machined to a curved cross section rather than being rectangular. The scalloped boards of the crossbeam and rafters served to cover the ends of the siding that met there. Though there is no direct counterpart in Gothic buildings, batten strip siding was a popular feature of architecture during the Gothic Revival and echoed the kind of soaring quality associated with the Gothic style.

The Kutztown Depot served the Philadelphia and Reading Railroad and was connected by a spur line to a main line linking the cities of Reading and Allentown and points beyond. Passenger service was discontinued in 1934. Freight service continued until 1976. The depot then housed an agricultural supply store until the store moved to larger quarters in 1990. Since that time the

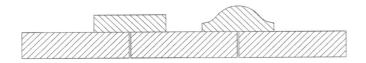

Cross sections of batten strips. Left, *a typical rectangular batten strip.* Right, *the machined, curved batten strips used on the Kutztown Depot.*

depot has been restored to its original appearance and belongs to the borough of Kutztown. It now is used for special events sponsored by community groups.

MAKING THE MINIATURE

The view of the station shown is the one train passengers would see on their arrival. Since this is the main side of the building, architects and historians would call it the "facade." This is the view used in most commercial miniature buildings. You will find other views in the projects that follow.

The first step in constructing the building is to make two photocopies of the drawing. One copy will be used for testing colors and rendering techniques, and the other copy will be used for the actual coloring and construction of the building. I would suggest that you have the photocopies made at a professional copying center where photocopying and printing are the major focus of the business rather than at an office supply store, library, or other business where photocopying is incidental to the business. A professional copying center will help you obtain the best possible print. Their machines usually are well maintained, and the glass platen is kept clean so that no specks of dirt will mar the photocopies.

The drawings shown in this book were made using fairly heavy lines so they would show up clearly when printed. You may find it desirable to have the photocopy lightened. Also, the photocopying center may have different weights of paper available. If so, try some of the heavier weights and ones with matte as well as gloss finishes. Sarah Grant (who does the color renderings for me) and I

The Kutztown Depot

> ### Use these colored pencils for the Kutztown Depot:
>
> - cloud blue
> - cool gray 20%
> - cool gray 50%
> - cream
> - dark brown
> - jade green
> - light cerulean blue
> - light umber
> - sienna brown
> - white
> - yellow ochre

found we preferred a paper with a very smooth surface because it gave a more solid appearance when colored than rough paper did.

Although the buildings in this book are drawn full-size, that is, the size they are intended to be made, you may want to change the size of the drawing for your own purposes when photocopying. Most copiers allow you to specify a certain amount of reduction or enlargement. For example, if the building you are copying is 7½ inches long and you want it to be only 6 inches long, you would divide 6 by 7½ to obtain the percentage you are seeking. In this example it would be 80 percent. Setting the copier to reduce to 80 percent of the original should give you the desired size. If you wanted to enlarge a drawing, you would divide the larger number by the smaller to get the amount of enlargement needed. For example, if the building you are copying is only 6 inches long and you want it to be 7½ inches long, you would divide 7½ by 6 and get 125 percent. You need to realize, however, that if you change the size of the drawing, you will also need to change the size of the block of wood specified in the text.

At this point some mention should be made of the scale to which the buildings were drawn. My original intention was to keep all of the buildings at the same scale with ³⁄₁₆ of an inch equaling 1 foot. For example, a door that was 8 feet tall in a building would be 1½ inches tall in the drawing. Sample buildings made to this scale showed me, however, that multistoried buildings visually overwhelmed the smaller, one-story buildings. As a consequence, I decided that no drawing of a building should be larger than 6 inches by 8 inches and that I would reduce the scale of a building to fit within these limits.

You will need a smooth surface for coloring the draw-ing of the railroad station. I use a piece of ⅛-inch clear acrylic, obtainable from most businesses that sell window glass. Before actually coloring a drawing, brush or wipe the surface of the acrylic so that it is free of sawdust or other particles that might interfere. Should you encounter them when coloring the building, the colored pencil will tend to deposit more color on the bump formed by the dirt under the paper than on the surrounding area, making it difficult to blend. So keep the surface under the drawing clean. And while we're talking about cleanliness, have a facial tissue or soft brush on hand to brush away small pieces of loose pigment that you may see on the surface of the drawing during the coloring process. Otherwise, they may end up where you don't want them and become embedded in the surface of the paper.

Coloring a building or any one of its details requires determining which colored pencils to use, in what order, and with what techniques. The illustration of coloring techniques for the Kutztown Depot (see color section) shows you the effects of each color on the previous one as you proceed through the sequence. Try each step first on one copy of the drawing to be sure you can achieve a color and texture similar to those shown. Once you are satisfied with your technique, you can repeat the process on the other photocopied drawing.

Coloring the Batten Strip Siding and Door Panels
Start by defining the batten strips. Sharpen the yellow ochre pencil to a fine point, and apply a line of color directly over the lines representing the batten strips. This will enhance the line and add a sense of shadow to the boards. You may find it difficult to apply this line of color evenly, but do not be too concerned—even its broken quality will help provide the desired emphasis to the batten strips. Sharpen the pencil frequently so that you can keep the shadow line to a barely visible width. Also apply the yellow ochre to the inner edges of the door panels, the scalloped edges along the crossbeam and the roof rafters, and the top of the sill across the bottom of the building. In fact, the yellow ochre shading should be applied to any intersection of the ends and edges of the siding with the framing surrounding it. In the finished drawing these shadow lines will help the siding to appear recessed behind the framing, thus contributing to the feeling of the way the building was constructed.

Work very carefully to keep the pencil point inside the

lines of the siding. If the strokes stray outside the area you are coloring, you will find them difficult to erase. Some books on using colored pencils advocate removing such errors by using an eraser or by scraping away the pigment with a knife blade. I have not been successful in doing either. As a matter of fact I don't try to erase errors anymore. Rather, I blend them in with the color of the adjacent area. Errors are inevitable and in their own way add something to the character of the work we create.

Using the cream-colored pencil and small, circular strokes, fill in each board in the siding. Your stroke should include covering the yellow ochre applied in the previous step. You will notice the yellow ochre blends into the cream, making a smooth transition between the batten strip and the siding. This is called "burnishing," a technique you will use frequently. When you have done all the siding, fill in the door panels with similar circular strokes. Burnish over the boards and door panels once again with the cream-colored pencil, but this time use vertical strokes paralleling the boards and the door panels.

Coloring the Windows

An interesting phenomenon concerning windows should be noted here. Although we know window glass is transparent, when we look at windows in a photograph or outdoors they frequently appear to be black. The few occasions that they appear to be some other color is when shades or curtains are drawn or there is a reflection from some other object. Curiously enough, if we make the windows of our drawings black, as they appear to be, they will visually overpower the rest of the drawing. Therefore, I usually make them a bluish gray color, like a cloudy sky, adding a little shading to give a sense of reflection to them.

You will be using crosshatching, diagonal and horizontal strokes, and burnishing techniques to shade the windowpanes. Crosshatching, as the term suggests, means to make a series of diagonal strokes and then go back over these strokes with a second set at right angles to the first.

Using the cloud blue pencil, fill in each windowpane separately with short, diagonal strokes, moving the pencil back and forth in a continuous motion. This will cause more pigment to be deposited at the edges of the panes, giving them a more precise form appropriate for windows. Be gentle, applying just sufficient pressure on the pencil to achieve a faint blush of color. Compare your efforts with the illustration, and modify your coloring technique as needed to achieve the desired effect. Repeat, using cloud blue with the same kind of strokes but at 90 degrees to the previous ones.

Apply the cool gray 20 percent pencil in short, diagonal strokes, only using slightly more pressure on the pencil so that the strokes are more pronounced. Fill in each windowpane separately.

Next, apply the jade green with a horizontal, continuous stroke. Keep the strokes light so that you achieve a sense of reflection of the sky in the windowpanes.

Once you have gotten the color of the panes as close as possible to those shown in the illustration, you can add shading around the upper and right edges of the panes with cool gray 50 percent in a soft, triangular shape. There should be no sharp edges. Then lighten the panes with white along the bottom and left edges. The white and the gray should blend into the underlying colors of the panes, again with no sharp edges.

Finally, sharpen the cool gray 50 percent pencil to a very fine point, and trace the mullions—the lines separating the windowpanes—along the bottom and right side of each line. Sharpen the white pencil to a very fine point, and trace along the top and left side of each line with the white pencil. This serves the same purpose as the yellow ochre used on the siding—to apply emphasis to the structure of the windows.

Coloring the Trim

Begin with a sharp-pointed light umber pencil, and fill in the framing members with short, lengthwise strokes, following the direction of each part. Apply the coat of pigment as evenly as you can.

Repeat the coloring of the trim with sienna brown, again using short, lengthwise strokes. When you finish with these colors, the trim should present a solid but not shiny surface. Go over the trim with the dark brown pencil, burnishing the colors together.

Coloring the Sign

The actual letters on the Kutztown sign are in white on a light blue background. I was unable to achieve this with my limited lettering techniques, and I settled for black lettering on a light blue background. Crosshatch the sign area with very light strokes of light cerulean blue. Be careful not to apply the color so heavily that you obscure the lettering on the sign. Follow with cloud blue, burnishing the darker blue in the same manner as when using dark brown to burnish the trim in the previous section.

At this point the coloring of the Victorian railroad station is complete. Compare your rendering of the building with both the photograph and the sample miniature building. Make any modifications or additions that might help improve the appearance of the building. Note areas where you experienced difficulty achieving a specific color quality, and try to determine how you might do it differently when you encounter a similar problem on subsequent projects. In general, if your coloring appears too dark, you have been pressing too hard on the colored pencils. If it appears too light, you have not been pressing hard enough. Experiment with the pressure on the pencils until your colors are very similar to those shown in the example.

Protecting the Drawing

When you are satisfied that you have colored the building as well as you can, apply two coats of fixative to the drawing. You will need to cover the workbench with newspaper to protect its surface from the spray fixative. Gently brush the surface of the drawing to remove loose particles of pigment and other dust and lay it, face up, on the newspaper. Follow the instructions given on the spray can, and apply an even coat of fixative to the drawing. Hold the can with the spray nozzle pointed toward the surface of the newspapers, off to one side of the drawing. Start moving the can toward the drawing and simultaneously press the spray button. The objective is to have the stream of spray moving horizontally before it reaches the surface of the drawing and to keep it moving until it has passed the far edge of the drawing, at which point you lift your finger from the spray button. This procedure will enable you to apply an even coat of spray to the drawing. You will need to make two or more overlapping passes of spray to ensure complete coverage. Be careful not to apply too much fixative, because that can create a frosted appearance. When finished, turn the spray can upside down, and press the spray button to clear the nozzle of fixative. I usually do this into an open space in the shop so that the spray settles on the floor, where it will be worn off quickly. When the drawing is dry, apply a second coat of fixative. Allow at least one hour of drying time between coats.

Cutting the Wood Block

The Kutztown Depot requires a block of wood measuring ¾ inch thick, 4½ inches wide, and 7½ inches long. The grain of the wood should run parallel to the long side of the block. (In some of the later buildings it will be necessary to orient the grain of the wood vertically, because structural features such as spires could easily break off if the grain of the wood ran parallel to the base of the building.)

With a try square and rule, draw a line across the board 7½ inches from one end, and cut it to this length. The best tool for cutting wood to the size needed for miniature buildings is a table saw. You also can use a handsaw, saber saw, or scroll saw. The table saw simply provides a cleaner cut as well as greater accuracy and ease of cutting. In the instructions that follow, I will assume you will be using a table saw and are familiar with its operation.

Make sure the saw's miter gauge is square to the saw blade, and use it to cut off the piece of wood to the length marked on the board. Next, set the fence on the saw to 4½ inches. Check the edges of the piece of wood just cut, place the best edge against the fence, and rip the wood to this width.

Rub the ends of the block of wood with sandpaper to remove splinters and tear-out. Then sand both the top and bottom faces of the block until the wood is smooth and free from surface defects. I like to use two grades of sandpaper, 100 grit followed by 150 grit. I prefer using garnet paper, but silicon carbide paper works just as well. I tear the paper into quarter sheets before using it. You can use either a sanding block or an electric pad sander to sand the surfaces of the board. Regardless of which you use, be careful not to round off the edges of the board. They should be kept crisp and square so that you will not encounter difficulties mounting the drawing on the wood during the next step.

Gluing the Drawing to the Wood Block

The next step requires the use of carbon paper. (If you do not have any, you can make your own. Take a small piece of plain paper—2 or 3 inches square—and, using a soft pencil, rub the edge of the lead, not the point, over the surface of the paper.) Place your carbon paper **face up** under the drawing centered directly beneath one of the corners of the rectangle surrounding the drawing of the

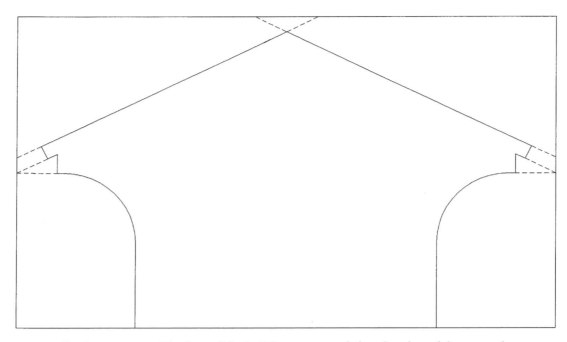

Cutting pattern. *The lines of the building are extended to the edges of the rectangle.*

building. Extend that corner outward ¼ to ½ inch, using a sharp pencil and a small straightedge. I use a small, clear acrylic triangle. Do this as precisely as possible since it will bear directly on how accurately you can attach the drawing to the wood block. Check the back of the photocopy. You should be able to see the corner extension lines. If they are not visible, it is probably because the piece of carbon paper was not face up or not centered under the corner. Redraw if necessary. Draw each of the remaining corner extensions in the same way. Turn the paper over and, using a straightedge and sharp pencil, connect the four corners of the rectangle. Check with the drawing on the front and write "bottom" or make small arrows or other markings to designate the bottom edge of the building on the back of the drawing. Place the wood block down on the rectangle. It should fit exactly within it. If not, determine where the problem lies and make any necessary corrections by resizing the piece of wood or retracing the rectangle on the back of the drawing. Extreme accuracy is not necessary here, but you want to be sure that the block is large enough to contain the building when one of its long edges is parallel to its bottom edge. The ends and top edge can be slightly longer or shorter, because they will eventually be trimmed away.

Draw a border about ½ inch larger on all sides than the rectangle and, using a straightedge and an X-acto

knife, cut away the excess paper using the border as a guide. The blade should be very sharp; otherwise you run the risk of tearing the paper. I use both a flat, diamond hone and a round, ceramic hone to maintain my knife blades. The diamond hone is good for use on blades with straight edges, and the ceramic hone works well on both straight and curved blades. Both hones can be purchased through mail-order woodworking stores. I also use a plastic cutting mat when cutting paper. The mat extends the life of the blades and protects the surface of the workbench. I bought mine at an art supply store.

Next, obtain a smooth, stiff piece of cardboard similar to that used for the back of writing tablets, and cut it about 2 inches greater in both length and width than the trimmed drawing of the building. Center the drawing **face down** on the cardboard, and tape its corners to the cardboard with small pieces of ½-inch-wide drafting tape. (Drafting tape is similar to masking tape but can be removed more easily from paper without tearing it. It is available from most art supply stores.) Be sure the tape doesn't extend over the rectangle drawn on the back. Smooth out the paper as you tape the corners so that it lies tightly against the surface of the cardboard. Next, tape down each edge of the drawing for its entire length. Again, be careful not to allow the tape to extend over the rectangle drawn on the back of the drawing. Allow at least ⅛ inch between the inner edges of the tape and the lines of the rectangle. In the next step you will be applying a spray adhesive to the back of the drawing; the use of drafting tape to hold the paper to the cardboard will prevent the spray propellant from lifting the paper and getting adhesive on the colored surface of the drawing.

Examine the long edges of the wood block. If one edge is better than the other—fewer nicks, scratches, or dents—mark that edge with a small piece of drafting tape.

The next steps are difficult, so proceed with great care. As a matter of fact, I suggest you make one or two trial runs before spraying the adhesive so that you understand how each step contributes to the task.

Tear four strips of drafting tape about an inch long and loosely attach them to the edge of the workbench in the area where you will be working so you can retrieve them easily when they are needed. Place the taped drawing, with the back of the drawing up, on newspapers on the workbench just as you did when applying fixative to the drawing. If you place it on a wooden block slightly smaller than the piece of cardboard, you will find it easier to pick up. Apply spray adhesive to the back of the drawing. Be sure you get an even coating over the entire surface of the paper.

Pick up the cardboard and drawing, and move them to where you have the tape strips. Lay the piece of cardboard down so that the marks on the drawing indicating the bottom edge of the building are facing you, and tape the corners of the cardboard to the workbench to prevent it from moving. Be careful that the tape does not overlap the lines of the rectangle on the back of the drawing. Pick up the wood block, holding it so that its bottom edge faces you with the back edge and the right end tilted slightly upward. Steady your hands against the surface of the workbench on either side of the cardboard, and slowly lower the wood block until the left corner just touches the sprayed surface exactly over the left corner mark on the back of the drawing. If your aim is poor, pick the block straight up from the drawing without disturbing the adhesive surface and reposition it on the back of the drawing. Once you have the left corner in place, and with the farthest edge still raised, gradually lower the right end of the wood block, keeping it aligned with the bottom edge line on the paper until its corner contacts the paper exactly at the right corner. Slowly lower the back edge of the block until it rests upon the paper.

Cut along the edges of the block with your knife. Take care not to cut into the workbench or the wood block. Remove the wood block from the piece of cardboard and examine it. If you have followed the process carefully, you should find that the bottom edge of the building coincides with the bottom edge of the wood block. It doesn't matter whether or not the other edges also coincide because they will be trimmed away when the building is cut out. Lay a clean sheet of paper on top of the drawing, and rub hard with your fingers to be sure the entire surface of the drawing is glued to the block of wood. Discard the trimmings as well as the piece of cardboard. I find it convenient to place a piece of scrap paper over the sticky paper to keep from getting adhesive on my hands. You can remove any adhesive you might have gotten on your hands with paint thinner. Wash well with soap and water afterward.

Study the drawing of the building and the cutting pattern provided. Since the building is symmetrical, each cut on one side of the building will be mirrored by the same cut on the other side. Use a straightedge and a sharp pencil to extend the lines of the roof until they intersect the sides and upper edges of the wood block. Extend the curves of the roof overhang to the outer edges of the block. Extend the bottom edges of the rafters outward until they meet the edges of the block.

Cutting the Outline of the Building

Install a new saw blade in the scroll saw, and adjust the table so the blade is perpendicular to it. If your saw has a variable speed control, set it to whatever speed you find works best. For cutting miniature buildings, I set my saw at about 1,200 strokes per minute. However, as the speed of a saw increases, there is a tendency to want to cut the wood faster, thereby increasing the possibility of errors. Consequently, you might want to use a somewhat slower speed for your first buildings.

You now are ready to cut out the building using two basic scroll saw techniques. The first cut is known as a *clear cut* and is the easiest one to make. It is used whenever you can cut along the outline of a building (such as the roof of the station) without having to make a second cut to remove the piece of waste wood. The cut can be a straight line, a curved line, or a combination of the two. The second cut is an *open, inside-corner cut.* It is used to cut a corner such as the one between the rafter and the outer edge of the overhang. This cut requires you to follow

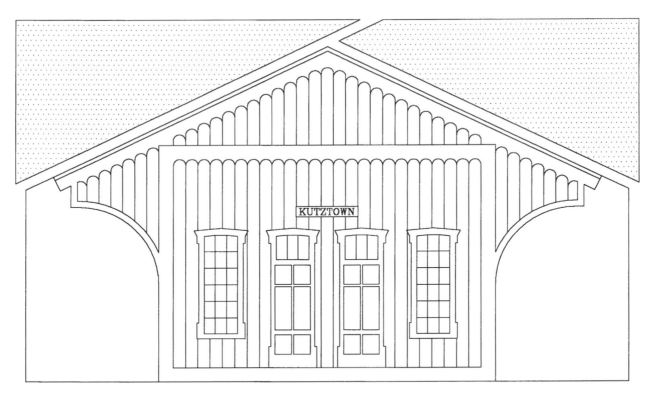

Cutting the roof. *Starting at one end of the wood block, a cut is made along one of the roof lines, removing that section of wood. The process is repeated for the second half of the roof.*

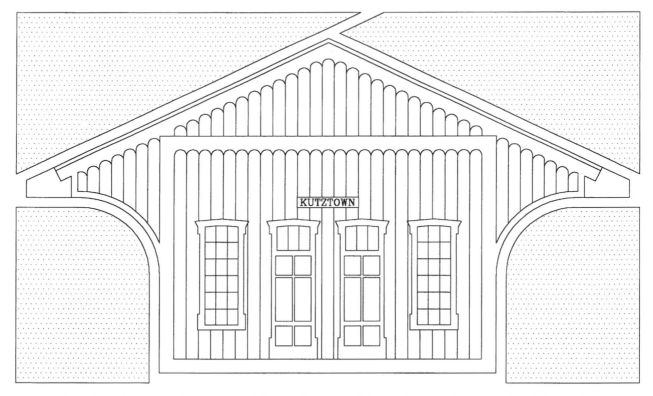

Cutting the sides. *A cut is made along one side and the curve of the overhang to the outer edge of the block. The second side is cut the same way.*

two different paths to remove the waste wood from the intersection. It is made by cutting along one line until it intersects the second line. With the saw running, the blade is backed out of the saw cut until it is free from the wood. (By keeping the saw turned on, you minimize the possibility that the saw blade will bind in the saw cut.) The second cut is made by following along the other line until it intersects the first line. The piece of waste wood should then be free from the block.

Starting at one end of the wood block, cut along one of the roof lines, removing that section of wood. If you find the blade wandering from the line, make gradual corrections until you are back on the line. Do not back up in the saw cut and restart unless the blade has wandered into the waste wood side of the line! If you do, the cutting error will appear much worse than if you make a gradual correction. However, if the saw cut has wandered into the waste wood, you can back up to where it left the line and very, very slowly resume cutting along the line until, once again, there is wood on both sides to help you guide the blade and finish the cut. After you have cut the waste wood from one side of the roof, repeat the process and cut along the second roof line.

Starting at the bottom edge of the wood block, cut along one side and the curve of the overhang until the outer edge of the block is met. Cut the second side and its overhang in the same way.

The next cut is an open, inside-corner cut in which the wood from between the bottom of the rafter and the upper end of the wall of the station is removed. Cut upward along the short end of the building between the arch and the edge of the rafter. Back out of the cut and then saw along the bottom edge of the rafter until you meet the line cut earlier. The piece of waste wood just cut should come free from the building. If it doesn't, saw just a bit past the end of the first cut, no more than 1/32 inch. If the scrap still doesn't come free, back out of the saw cut and resaw the first cut. Again, go slightly past the end of the other line, if necessary, to free the scrap of wood. Repeat these steps and cut away the waste wood on the other side. Finally, trim the ends of the two rafters.

Notice that in cutting out the train station, each cut began with the blade as close as possible to a right angle with the edge of the wood. For example, you started the cut along the roof line from an end of the wood block rather than from the top edge because the line was closer

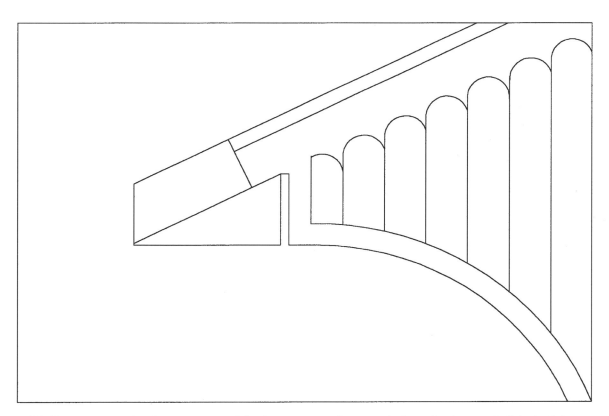

Making an open, inside-corner cut. *The first cut is made upward along the short end of the building.*

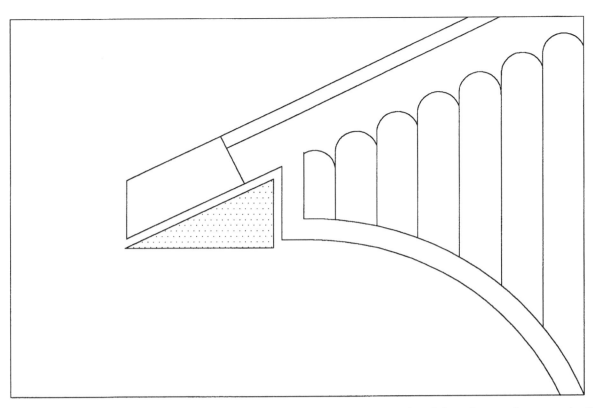

Making an open, inside-corner cut. *The second cut is made along the bottom edge of the rafter until it meets the first cut.*

Cutting the ends of the rafters. *Trimming the rafters finishes the cutting of the Kutztown Depot.*

TROUBLE WITH THE SAW?

If you had difficulty cutting the waste wood free from the inside-corner cut, there are two probable causes. First, your saw blade may not be square to the table, so the two cuts did not meet at the bottom of the intersection. If this is the problem, readjust the saw table. Second, you may be pressing the wood to one side or the other while cutting, forcing the blade to cut at an angle. If this latter problem should be the case, you will need to be aware of it as you cut other buildings. Hold the piece of wood down with a light pressure, just sufficient to keep it from getting caught in the teeth of the saw blade, and move the block of wood squarely into the saw blade by applying pressure to the edge of the wood opposite the saw cut. If the piece of wood is caught in the teeth of the saw blade, it will be wrenched from your hands and will bounce up and down with some force.

Even if the open, inside-corner cut was successful, you should turn the building upside down and examine the two intersections. The two cut lines should just meet. If they extend beyond the corner of the intersection, either the blade is not square to the table, or you are pressing the saw blade out of alignment to the left or right.

to a right angle there. It is much easier to begin a cut accurately when the blade approaches the line at a right angle with the edge of the wood. If you start a cut at a shallow angle, the saw blade will take the path of least resistance and tend to skitter or bounce off the edge of the wood rather than bite into it. This makes it difficult to start exactly on the line to be cut. When it does become necessary to make a shallow angle cut, hold the piece of wood tightly as you are approaching the wood, and feed it very slowly into the blade until the cut is started exactly where you want it.

When you have completed cutting out the building, sand the cut edges to remove any splinters, burrs, or tear-out. I use one-eighth of a sheet of 150-grit sandpaper, folding it several times until it is small enough to fit into corners such as the recesses under the eaves. You can round the edges slightly on the back of the wood so that they are not sharp to the touch. If some of your cutting errors are more than can be removed with abrasive paper, use a smoothing file to remove them.

Finishing

After the building has been sanded, the bare wood should be given two coats of wood sealer. Stir the sealer well, and apply it to the edges of the building with a small brush. Try not to get any of it on the front of the building. If you do—and you will—wipe it off with your bare finger and then wipe the sealer from your finger onto a paper towel or a piece of cloth. The sealer dries rapidly, so be sure to check the front of the building frequently and remove at once any sealer that has crept over the edges. Wash the sealer out of your brush by swishing it up and down in the jar of thinner several times, and then wipe it dry on a clean piece of paper. Do this two or three times and the brush will be ready to use for applying a coat to the back of the building. Allow the sealer coat to dry on the edges before applying it to the back of the building. After this coat has dried, sand it lightly with 150-grit sandpaper to remove any of the grain that may have been raised by the sealer. Apply a second coat to the edges and back of the building in the same way. Again, sand lightly after the sealer has thoroughly dried.

Once the wood has been sealed and sanded, the edges and back of the building should be painted in a color that harmonizes with the colors used for the building itself. You will need to experiment with mixing colors, putting samples on a piece of paper and noting their color after they have dried. Most colors tend to dry darker. Also, when mixing colors, begin with a light color and add the darker colors to it. You will find with experience that it requires just a bit of dark color to darken one that is light but an awful lot of a light color to lighten one that is too dark.

For the Kutztown Depot, I used white, yellow, and burnt umber to create a light cream color similar to that of the cream-colored pencil. Begin by placing about one teaspoonful of white in a small container. (Baby food jars are great for this purpose because their lids can be pressed back on to keep the paint from drying out when it is not being used.) Add a few drops of yellow and a drop of burnt

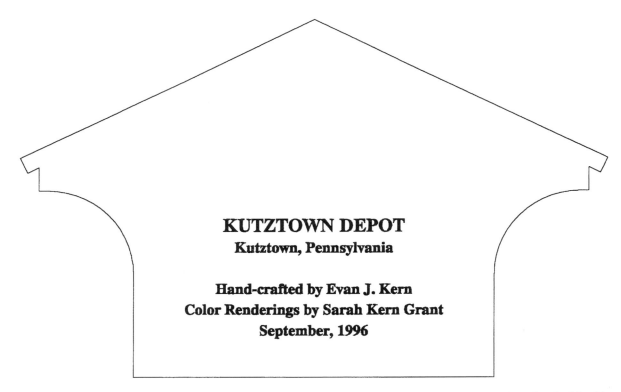

KUTZTOWN DEPOT
Kutztown, Pennsylvania

Hand-crafted by Evan J. Kern
Color Renderings by Sarah Kern Grant
September, 1996

Label for the miniature Kutztown Depot. An informative, transparent label is put on the back of the finished building. The back also is initialed with a pen.

umber to the white, and stir until well mixed. A small, thin piece of wood like a Popsicle stick makes a good stirrer. Compare the color of the mixture to the cream-colored sample (see color section), and add more of whichever color seems to be needed to obtain the proper shade. When you have mixed a color that you think will be satisfactory, add a few drops of flow improver and mix thoroughly.

Use a ½-inch, acrylic or watercolor cut-end brush (a cut-end brush is one in which the ends of the bristles are cut off in a straight line) to apply the paint to the edges and back of the miniature building. Paint the edges first and then, when they have dried, the back. As with the sealer coats, be careful not to get any of the paint on the front of the building. If you do, wipe it off quickly. Acrylic paint tends to act like glue when it dries, so be sure to support the building off the surface of the workbench on a small piece of wood while the paint dries. When you have finished applying the first coat of paint, wash the brush thoroughly in soap and water, rinse well, and reshape the bristles by gently pulling them between your thumb and forefinger.

After the first coat of paint has dried, sand it lightly with 150-grit abrasive paper, and then apply a second coat to the edges and back. Again, wash and reshape the brush.

While the paint dries, you might want to make a label for the building. I write the name of the building, its location, the year of its construction, my name, and the date the miniature was made. I type this information on a transparent label and then put it in place on the back of the building. I also sign my initials on the back of the building in waterproof ink.

Your miniature Victorian railroad station is now finished. You can display it on a mantel, shelf, windowsill, or anywhere else it can be seen to advantage.

You now know the fundamental processes and techniques used to make miniature wooden buildings. You have learned how to use colored pencils to achieve the color and texture of a building with batten strip siding. You have learned to glue the drawing to a block of wood and cut it out with a scroll saw. Finally, you have learned to mix and apply acrylic paint to the edges and back of the building. With these skills you are ready to tackle a building constructed quite differently from the Victorian railroad station—the Fisher-Martin House.

3
THE FISHER-MARTIN HOUSE

I chose the Fisher-Martin House for the second project because it provides several challenges not found in the Victorian railroad station. In contrast to the first project, this building is drawn from a three-quarter, or perspectival, view.

The Fisher-Martin House was built in Cool Spring, Delaware, in about 1730. The tract upon which this house was built was owned in 1695 by Thomas Fisher, a wealthy merchant. It was sold by his son in 1736, to Reverend James Martin, a minister in Cool Spring, and remained in the Martin family for over 200 years. It was moved to Lewes, Delaware, in 1980, and it currently houses the Lewes Chamber of Commerce.

The house is built in the Anglo-Dutch tradition—that is, it possesses stylistic qualities from both England and the Low Countries (formerly Holland and Flanders, now Netherlands, Belgium, and Luxembourg). Distinguished by its gambrel roof, the Fisher-Martin House represents a style of American architecture that combined the tradition of the English medieval manor house with that of Flanders. With its lower, steep sections and upper, flatter sections, the design provides more headroom in the rooms directly beneath. In earlier versions of this style, the break of the gambrel in the roof is just below the ridgeline; the break became much lower in later versions. This style of roof can be found on both houses and barns throughout the mid-Atlantic region.

MAKING THE MINIATURE

Because the house is drawn from a three-quarter view, structural features such as the siding, which would be parallel in a front view, are no longer parallel. This means that the boards of the siding, as well as other features of the building, gradually become smaller the farther they are from the viewer. This doesn't present a problem when col-oring most of the house, but it will need to be taken into consideration when coloring the roof and chimney. Also, since the bottom edges of a building drawn in perspective do not form a straight line, it is necessary to form a base below the bottom edges of the building so that it will stand up. This base is interpreted as the ground and, for this building, is colored to appear as grass.

The weathered wood of the Fisher-Martin House will provide you with a challenge in using a wide variety of colors to simulate the weathering effect. Review the information given in the previous chapter about photocopying and coloring buildings with colored pencils before starting to color a photocopy of the Fisher-Martin House. Again, I

USE THESE COLORED PENCILS FOR THE FISHER-MARTIN HOUSE:

- apple green
- blue gray
- cool gray 20%
- cool gray 50%
- cream
- crimson red
- dark brown
- dark green
- dark purple
- French gray 50%
- indigo
- jade green
- light umber
- lilac
- peach
- periwinkle
- sepia
- sienna brown
- terra cotta
- Tuscan red
- warm gray 20%
- warm gray 50%
- warm gray 70%
- white

The Fisher-Martin House

recommend making two photocopies of the drawing so that you can use one to experiment with various coloring techniques.

Coloring the Siding

1. Apply warm gray 50 percent unevenly over all of the walls, leaving some areas lighter than others.

2. Apply sepia in short, jagged strokes just in spots of the siding to simulate the grain of wood. Repeat in other areas of the siding, using dark brown first, and then light umber.

3. Apply warm gray 20 percent unevenly, heavier in some areas than others.

4. Use warm gray 70 percent to form shadows on the bottom edges of the boards.

5. Apply blue gray with light, diagonal, spaced strokes over all of the walls. Repeat, using indigo in light, diagonal strokes.

6. Use sienna brown and peach to create warmer areas on the siding.

Coloring the Door and Trim

1. Apply crimson red lightly and evenly to the door, window frames, and door frame.

2. Apply Tuscan red lightly to the window and door frames. Apply the same color to the door using light, diagonal strokes.

3. Repeat the previous step using carmine red; then sharpen the pencil and draw vertical stripes on the door to simulate the boards from which it was constructed.

4. Burnish the frames and door with peach.

5. Use blue gray followed by dark purple to create the shadow areas.

Coloring the Windows

1. Apply cool gray 20 percent to the upper left corner of each windowpane.

2. Apply cool gray 50 percent to the lower right corner of each windowpane.

3. Apply just a touch of periwinkle to the center area of each windowpane.

4. Burnish each windowpane with a white pencil.

Coloring the Roof

The roof is covered with wood shingles that will need to be drawn at the same time as they are colored. When shingles are applied to a roof, they are placed in straight, overlapping rows and frequently have ragged lower edges. In a perspectival view, however, the rows at the far end of the roof appear to be closer together than at the near end. This may give you some difficulty as you attempt to space the rows. One solution is to draw guidelines very lightly on the roof.

To determine where to draw these lines, you will have to locate the *vanishing point* from which the roof was drawn. The term "vanishing point" is used in perspective drawing to indicate where all the lines from a particular view converge. For example, if you look down a long, straight highway, the two sides of the road will appear to meet on the far horizon. This is the vanishing point. The phenomenon is a consequence of our binocular vision (seeing with two eyes) that enables us to distinguish between things that are near to us from things that are farther away. The near objects appear larger, the far objects, smaller, even though the near thing—an automobile—may be small in comparison to the far thing—a mountain.

My explanation is oversimplified but should serve to help find the vanishing point. Tape the drawing to a larger piece of paper so that the right edge of the paper is at least 10 inches from the right edge of the drawing. (Use drafting tape so that you can remove the drawing later without damaging it.) Lay a straightedge or ruler exactly along the bottom line of the roof and, using a pencil, extend it off the right edge of the paper about 10 inches. Repeat, this time extending the line in the middle of the roof. The two lines should intersect about 9 inches from the edge of the rectangle surrounding the house. This intersection is the vanishing point. Mark it with a short vertical line running through the center of the intersection.

Using a pencil having a hard lead, such as 4H or 5H, divide the upper edge of the left end of the gable into about six spaces and the lower gable edge into eight spaces. Make very small, light marks. Align the edge of a straight-edge so that it just touches both the first mark and the vanishing point and draw a light line the length of the roof. Repeat with the subsequent marks on both the lower and upper roof sections. Do not draw lines through the chimney.

You will discover that there is an even progression of spaces between the lines, their being closer together at the right end of the roof than at the left end. The vertical lines needed to distinguish individual shingles could be drawn in the same way but from a vanishing point above the roof. I don't believe you will find it necessary, however, since the two gable ends are practically parallel to one another.

Now you are ready to color the roof.
1. Apply warm gray 20 percent with short, zigzag strokes to each row of shingles.
2. Apply French gray 50 percent in short strokes that parallel the roof angle to define individual shingles.
3. Burnish with white, using fine, zigzag strokes.
4. Sharpen the point of the blue gray pencil and repeat step 2. Then go over all the lower roof section with light strokes paralleling the roof angle.
5. Apply spots of jade green and lilac very lightly in the corners and in the shadow around the base of the chimney.
6. Color the gable ends of the roof using the same pencils used for the shingles. Some areas should be darker than others to simulate the weathering process.

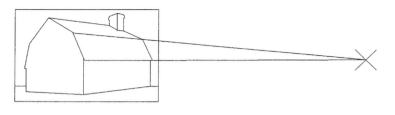

Locating the vanishing point. *The horizontal lines of the roof are extended to the right until they meet. This is called the vanishing point.*

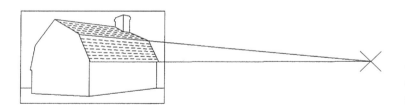

Locating the rows of shingles. *Light pencil lines are drawn from the vanishing point to the left edge of the roof to locate the rows of shingles.*

Coloring the Chimney

1. Sharpen the terra cotta pencil and apply crosshatching lightly over the entire area.

2. Sharpen the terra cotta pencil again and apply crosshatching over the entire area. This time, however, begin forming the individual bricks with the crosshatching.

3. Apply Tuscan red in diagonal strokes on the left side of the chimney to create a shadow.

4. Burnish the areas above and to the left of each brick with light, horizontal strokes using the peach pencil.

5. Burnish each brick with light, crosshatched strokes using the cream-colored pencil. Repeat with the peach.

6. Use dark purple in light, parallel strokes under the decorative band of bricks on the chimney to further define it.

Coloring the Lawn

1. Use crosshatching to apply blue gray to the entire lawn area. Begin by coloring with light, diagonal strokes. Turn the paper 90 degrees, and complete the crosshatching by making light, diagonal strokes at right angles to the first. Follow by crosshatching with peach, cream, jade green, and apple green.

2. Make tufts of grass with dark green.

When you have finished coloring the house, apply two coats of fixative.

Cutting

Review the previous chapter's discussion on attaching the drawing to the wood before taking the next steps.

1. Using carbon paper, draw the extensions of the corners on the back of the drawing and then connect the corners to form the rectangle surrounding the house.

2. Tape the drawing, face down, on a piece of cardboard.

3. Cut a block of wood 4 inches by 6 inches; sand its front, back, and edges.

4. Apply spray adhesive to the back of the drawing, and position the wood block on it.

5. Trim the excess paper from around the edges of the wood block.

6. Draw extension lines from the roof, eaves, and chimney as shown.

In cutting out this building you will make extensive use of the *closed, inside-corner cut,* because none of the corners on the outline of the house are accessible with a straight or open corner cut. Begin by cutting out the waste wood on the left end of the block between the upper edge of the lawn and the lower edge of the eave. Install a new blade in the saw, and then cut along the line of the eaves until you just meet the wall of the house. Back the saw out of this cut, and then cut along the upper edge of the lawn until, again, you reach the wall of the house. Back the saw about halfway out of the cut, and start sawing upward in an arc

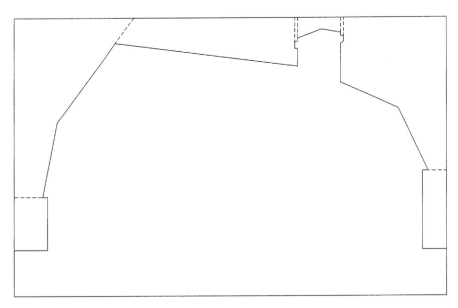

Cutting pattern for the Fisher-Martin House. *Extension lines are drawn from the roof, eaves, and chimney.*

Making a closed, inside-corner cut. The first cut is from the edge of the wood along the eave line to the edge of the house.

Making a closed, inside-corner cut. The second cut is along the upper edge of the lawn until it meets the edge of the house. The saw is partially backed out of the cut, and then a curving cut is made to meet the edge of the house. The cutting is continued along the edge of the house until it meets the first cut.

Making a closed, inside-corner cut. *The third cut removes the small triangle of wood left in the corner between the lawn and the edge of the house.*

that will intersect the wall of the house about ½ inch from the bottom corner. Saw along this line until you meet the saw cut under the eave. The piece of waste wood should come free from the building. If not, review the discussion about this in the previous chapter. To finish the inside, closed-corner cut, turn the piece of wood around 180 degrees, and cut along the line of the wall until you meet the saw cut along the top edge of the lawn. Take your time making this cut so that the edge of the house looks as if it were made with one continuous cut. Just gradually nibble away at the excess wood with the edge of the saw blade parallel to the line to be cut. The edge of the wood will eventually be wide enough that the saw blade will have wood on both sides, making it easier to control. The piece of waste wood at the opposite end of the house can be cut out in the same way.

Beginning at the top edge of the block of wood, cut the end of the left gable. The change in direction between the two sections of the roof should present no problem. Slow up as you approach the intersection, and gradually turn the piece of wood until the saw blade lines up with the second line. Then cut along it until you meet the eave.

The cuts between the chimney and its intersection with the roof, as well as the intersection between the outer edge of the chimney and the extended row of bricks around the chimney near its upper edge, are cut the same way. Begin by cutting along the outer extension line of the chimney to cut the edge of the decorative band of bricks around the chimney, and then gradually curve inward until the saw blade meets the edge of the chimney. Cut along this line until it meets the chimney's intersection with the roof. Back out of the cut. Beginning at the opposite end of the roof line, cut along it until the blade meet its intersection with the chimney. The piece of waste wood should come free at this point. Repeat the process to cut away the wood from the other side of the chimney and roof.

Cut along one of the upper sides of the decorative band of bricks until the blade intersects the edge of the chimney. Back out of the cut. Then cut from the top edge downward along the inner extension line of the chimney until you meet the line just cut. Repeat on the other side of the chimney.

Cut along one of the undersides of the decorative band of bricks until the blade meets the edge of the chim-

Cutting the gable of the gambrel roof. *Both edges of the gable are sawed with one continuous cut.*

Cutting the roof ridge and chimney. *The first cut is made just past the decorative band of the chimney and then follows the edge of the chimney until it meets the roof ridge.*

Cutting the roof ridge and chimney. *The second cut is made along the ridge until it meets the intersection with the first cut. The third cut trims the wood around the decorative band of the chimney.*

ney. Back out of the cut. Then back into the corner between the edge of the chimney and the roof, and trim away the piece of wood remaining from the initial closed corner cut. Repeat the cut on the other side of the chimney. Cut the upper edges of the chimney, and trim the end of the right eave to complete the cutting.

Finishing

Sand the edges and back of the house in preparation for applying sealer to the bare wood. Apply two coats of sealer, sanding after each coat has dried.

When you made the Victorian railroad station, you painted the edges and back all the same color. With the Fisher-Martin House you are going to paint some of the edges one color and other edges different colors to enhance the three-dimensional quality of the building. To do this you will need to mix one color for the edges adjoining the roof, another for the edges and top of the chimney, a third for the edges adjoining the walls, and a fourth for the edges adjoining the lawn. You will paint the back of the house the

same color as the edges adjoining the roof—a light silver gray. Mix that color of paint first.

Pour about 1 teaspoonful of white into your mixing container, and add a drop of black. Stir well and compare the color on the stirring stick to the light silver gray shown on the paint sample (see color section). If it is too dark, add some white; if it is too light, add some black. This color will dry darker, so make your mix slightly lighter than it appears on the sample. When you think you have matched the color sample, then paint the edges on the right side of the building from the lawn up to the bottom edge of the chimney. Paint the edges on the left side of the building from the base of the chimney to the lawn. Keep a constant check for paint on the front of the building, wiping away any that you find. Put the house aside to dry. Cover your paint container so that the paint will not dry out.

Meanwhile, mix the color for the lawn—a grass green. Again, begin with white and add a drop each of green, blue, and yellow. Mix well and compare to the paint sample. Lighten or darken as needed. If the color seems too turquoise or blue, add yellow. If it appears too yellow, add either green or blue, according to the appearance of the yellow. When you are satisfied with the color of the paint, and when you are sure the gray paint has dried, apply the paint to the top edges and ends of the lawn.

While the lawn is drying, mix the brick red for the chimney. Start with the white paint, and add a drop or two of oxide red. Mix well and compare your color to the color sample. If it is too light, add a drop of red (not oxide red). If it appears too red, add a drop of yellow. Again, remember this color will dry darker. When the color appears to be correct, paint the edges and top of the chimney.

After the paint on all of the edges has dried, you can paint the back of the house with the light silver gray you mixed earlier. Holding the building by the edges, apply the paint from the center outward. This will help keep the gray from getting on the green of the lawn and the red of the chimney. Place face down on a small square of wood to dry. Allow to dry overnight before applying a second coat to all the edges and the back, using the same colors and following the sequence given above.

Label the building with whatever information you choose, and your Fisher-Martin House is finished. Reflect upon your experience making the building. What were the hardest parts? Making the inside-corner cuts? If so, practice making some on the scrap wood left over from making the house and the railroad station. Was the hardest part coloring the house? Coloring the shingles? If so, make another photocopy and experiment with the colors until you achieve the qualities you seek.

4

SAINT PETER'S PARISH HALL

You find some wonderful buildings simply by chance. Saint Peter's Parish Hall is one of them. My wife and I were on a trip through Delaware and Maryland photographing buildings for this project. We stopped in Smyrna, Delaware, for lunch, picking a restaurant simply because it had been open for as many years as I have been alive. The waitress mentioned that there were really nice buildings in Smyrna's historic district and that there were drawings of some of the buildings in the bar in the restaurant. We took a look at the drawings, saw the parish hall, and headed out to find it.

The construction of the parish hall is similar to that of the Kutztown Depot with several Gothic Revival features. Among these are the steep, sloping gables of the main building, the entryway, and the enclosed porch; the Gothic arch surrounding the door; the batten strips with their unique Gothic arches under the gable; and the rose window over the door with its delicate tracery. The brilliant red doors of the entryway in contrast to the white and blue grays of the main structure make a focal point for the building. All in all, it is a very attractive parish hall, considered by some to be one of the finest examples of Carpenter Gothic in the state of Delaware.

Saint Peter's Church in Smyrna is one of the oldest in the Episcopal Diocese of Delaware. It was established in 1704 by Reverend Thomas Crawford, the first missionary to Kent County. The parish hall was built as a Sunday school in 1872 and originally was referred to as the "chapel."

MAKING THE MINIATURE

From this point on, all of the projects in the book follow the same coloring processes as described in rendering the Victorian railroad station and the Fisher-Martin House. The only things that will change are the specific colored pencils and techniques needed for coloring particular elements of a building. Therefore, refer to the previous chapters if you don't recall the steps to follow at any stage of the coloring.

Prepare for coloring the parish hall by making two photocopies of the drawing of the building.

Coloring the Siding

You may think that coloring the boards of the parish hall is an exercise in futility since they are white like the paper of the drawing. However, if you fail to do so, or if you miss coloring one of the boards, the paper will someday begin to darken from age, and any board without the white pigment will become darker than the surrounding areas of white.

1. Color each board separately using short, diagonal strokes of white in one direction only.

2. Repeat with diagonal strokes at right angles to the first.

3. Finish with medium-length vertical strokes, burnishing all of the white together.

USE THESE COLORED PENCILS FOR THE PARISH HALL:

- blue gray
- cloud blue
- cool gray 20%
- cool gray 50%
- cool gray 70%
- geranium lake
- imperial purple
- indigo
- jade green
- madder carmine
- periwinkle
- rose madder lake
- rose pink
- spectrum orange
- straw yellow
- warm gray 70%
- water green
- white

Saint Peter's Parish Hall

Hold the paper so a light source, such as daylight through a window, strikes it at an angle. If you missed any of the boards they will show up as a flat, dull white rather than the shiny pencil white. Color any boards you missed.

Coloring the Batten Strips

1. Begin by coloring each strip with the cool gray 50 percent, following the contours of the strips under the eaves and using straight-line strokes to fill in the vertical strips between each board. Go over the battens at least twice to ensure complete coverage. Keep your pencil sharp when doing the thin battens separating the boards.

2. Burnish over the gray with white. Again, keep the pencil point sharp when doing the thin battens.

Coloring the Trim

1. Begin with a light coat of warm gray 70 percent, and color all the trim strips, including the outer frame of the rose window. Apply the color in straight or curved lines as necessary to fill in the spaces.

2. Follow this coloring with indigo, again applying the color with very light strokes.

3. Apply blue gray in the same way, and then burnish over all using white.

4. Add more indigo and cool gray 70 percent to the trim, following with just a trace of periwinkle.

5. Shade the trim under the eaves with cool gray 50 percent and more periwinkle.

6. Burnish all with another coat of white.

Coloring the Doors

1. Apply madder carmine with short, vertical strokes over the entire area of the entryway.

2. Apply indigo with vertical strokes only in shadow areas.

3. Apply geranium lake, again with vertical strokes over all of the entryway.

4. Apply geranium lake with diagonal strokes.

5. Burnish the colors with white, using vertical strokes.

6. Apply geranium lake with crosswise strokes, followed by vertical strokes.

7. Apply madder carmine, using both diagonal and horizontal strokes.

8. Apply imperial purple in areas of shadow, using vertical strokes.

9. Apply straw yellow to the doorknobs.

Coloring the Steps

1. Apply warm gray 70 percent to the edges of the steps in thin, horizontal lines.

2. Apply cool gray 50 percent to the face of the steps, again using horizontal lines.

3. Shade under each step with periwinkle, concentrating most of the color in the upper corners and working from the ends inward.

4. Repeat the shading, this time with imperial purple.

Coloring the Rose Window

The rose window needs to be colored so that it simulates a stained-glass window. Coloring it is one of the most interesting and creative challenges in the book. Let yourself go—but not so much that the window overpowers the rest of the building.

1. Apply a light coat of cool gray 20 percent over all the frame, using diagonal strokes.

2. Use cool gray 50 percent to delineate the outer area of the inner frame.

3. Use cool gray 70 percent for the openings in the inner frame.

4. Shade the upper portions of the frame with cloud blue.

5. Use periwinkle to further define the shading.

Use the following steps to color the individual windowpanes of the rose window. (Study the rendering of the building in the color section.)

1. Apply cool gray 50 percent very lightly in the upper left area of each pane.

2. Apply cool gray 50 percent around the center of the rose window to form a small, soft-edged circle. Do not get the color on the mullions between the panes.

3. Apply water green very, very lightly in diagonal strokes to give just a hint of the color.

4. Use rose pink, rose madder lake, jade green, and spectrum orange to create the effect of a stained-glass window. You may want to add some colors of your own choice. Just remember to be restrained.

Apply two coats of fixative to the drawing as described in chapter 2.

Cutting and Finishing

Instead of repeating the instructions for cutting out the wooden building, I will simply give you a list of the steps to be followed. If you have forgotten how to do some of them, return to the instructions in chapter 2.

1. Cut a piece of wood 5½ inches square, and sand the back and edges.

2. Mark the corner extensions, and draw the square surrounding the parish hall on the back of the drawing.

3. Trim the drawing; tape it to a piece of cardboard.

4. Spray adhesive on the back of the drawing, and place the wood block in position on the square.

5. Trim excess paper from around the wood block, and rub the surface of the drawing to be sure it is well glued to the block.

6. Draw the extension lines from the building to the edges of the wood block.

7. Cut out the building. You should have no difficulty doing this because it is simpler than the previous buildings.

8. Sand and apply two coats of sealer to the edges and the back of the building. Sand after each coat dries.

9. Mix white, blue, and black to approximate the color of the trim of the building. Compare the color you mix to the color sample (see color section) for dark blue gray. Apply two coats of the paint to the edges and back, sanding between coats.

10. Label and sign the building on the back.

You have finished the construction of Saint Peter's Parish Hall. Our next project, a lawyer's office, presents a new set of challenges.

5

LAWYER'S OFFICE

Built in Cambridge, Maryland, circa 1820, this small, frame office building is Federal in style. The Federal features include the dentil beam along the cornice, a semicircular fan light with a ray pattern above the door, and the pilaster columns on either side of the door. (The dentil beam with its series of rectangular blocks predates classical Greek architecture and derives its design from the ends of wooden beams in earlier forms of construction.) The office contains two rooms linked by a central entryway, a floor plan similar to that of the manor houses in Tudor England.

The Federal period of architecture in the United States occurred mainly between 1790 and 1830. In many respects it represents an extension of the Georgian style; the only notable difference in domestic architecture is one of size, American Federal homes being substantially larger than their earlier Georgian counterparts. The Federal style was applied to buildings other than homes, this lawyer's office being but one example. You will encounter another in the New Castle Old Town Hall in Delaware.

It was not unusual to find small, specialized office buildings in rural areas. In addition to a lawyer's office such as this, one might also find one-room doctor's and surveyor's offices. These buildings were inexpensive to build and maintain and allowed lawyers, doctors, and surveyors to perform their services in remote areas. Later you will be making a miniature surveyor's office.

MAKING THE MINIATURE

You should meet few difficulties in coloring this building, the coloring of the chimney and brick foundation being the most challenging. Prepare for coloring the building by making two photocopies of the drawing.

Coloring the Siding

1. Color each of the boards of the siding with cream. Use horizontal strokes.

2. Use the French gray 20 percent to shade the siding. Concentrate the color along the upper edge of each board. The outside of the lawyer's office is covered with German siding. This siding has a curved upper edge that fits into a notch cut in the bottom edge of the board above for weathertight construction. This curved recess stands out rather sharply, especially when in shadow.

Coloring the Trim, Door, and Window Frames

1. Apply the smalt blue and periwinkle in straight lines following the direction of the various parts of the trim and frames of the door and windows. Leave the dentils under the eaves slightly lighter than the cornice board.

2. Use the blue slate pencil to add shadows along the right side of each dentil.

USE THESE COLORED PENCILS FOR THE LAWYER'S OFFICE:

- blue gray
- blue slate
- cloud blue
- cool gray 20%
- cool gray 70%
- cream
- French gray 20%
- French gray 70%
- imperial purple
- indigo
- jade green
- light peach
- orange
- peach
- periwinkle
- smalt blue
- terra cotta
- Tuscan red
- warm gray 70%

Lawyer's office

Coloring the Door

1. Apply French gray 70 percent in both vertical and horizontal strokes following the lines of the door and door panels. Follow the direction of the individual panes when doing the fan window above the door.

Design of German siding. This siding has a curved upper edge, which fits into a notch cut in the bottom edge of the board above for weathertight construction.

2. Burnish the door frame, panels, and fan window with the cream-colored pencil.

3. Use warm gray 70 percent to apply shading to the fan window.

4. Apply warm gray 70 percent in light, diagonal strokes to the door frame and panels to provide textural relief.

Coloring the Windows

1. Using a sharp, cool gray 70 percent pencil and light, diagonal strokes, color in each windowpane.

2. Using a cloud blue pencil with a very blunt point, add shading to the upper left corners of the windowpanes.

3. Apply jade green very lightly to the shading of the windowpanes. Add a few light, diagonal strokes in other areas of the window.

4. Use the cream-colored pencil to lighten the color in the lower right corners of the windowpanes.

Coloring the Roof

With this roof you do not have to define the individual shingles, since they already have been drawn.

1. Apply blue gray to the entire roof area, using short, horizontal strokes. Follow with cool gray 70 percent and cool gray 20 percent, using the same kind of strokes.

2. Apply jade green with short, diagonal strokes.

3. Apply indigo very lightly, with diagonal strokes at right angles to those used in the previous step.

4. Use imperial purple with light, short, diagonal strokes to shade the area below the base of the chimney.

Coloring the Chimney and Foundation

1. Sharpen the peach pencil, and lightly apply crosshatching over the entire area.

2. Sharpen the terra cotta pencil, and apply crosshatching over the entire area. This time, however, begin forming the individual bricks with crosshatching.

3. Use Tuscan red and make the edges of the bricks more precise by using vertical strokes on the ends and horizontal strokes along the bottom edges.

4. Burnish the areas above and to the left of each brick with light, horizontal strokes of light peach.

5. Burnish each brick with light, crosshatched strokes with the orange pencil. Use orange in horizontal strokes under the decorative band of bricks on the chimney to further define it.

Coloring the Steps

1. Apply cool gray 70 percent to the edges and faces of the steps with short, horizontal strokes. The color should be heavier toward the ends of the steps and lighter toward the centers.

2. Apply French gray 20 percent to the face of the steps, again using horizontal lines. Apply most of the color to the center area of the steps.

3. Shade under each step with periwinkle, concentrating most of the color in the upper corners and working in from the ends.

4. Repeat the shading with imperial purple.

Apply two coats of fixative when satisfied with coloring.

Cutting and Finishing

Instead of repeating the instructions for cutting out the wooden building, I will simply give you a list of the steps to be followed. If you have forgotten some of the procedures, refer to the instructions in chapter 2.

1. Cut a piece of wood 4 inches by 6¼ inches, and sand the back and edges.

2. Mark the corner extensions, and draw the square surrounding the lawyer's office on the back of the drawing.

3. Trim the drawing; tape it to a piece of cardboard.

4. Spray adhesive on the back of the drawing, and place the wood block in position on the square.

5. Trim the excess paper from around the wood block, and rub the drawing to be sure it is well glued to the block.

6. Draw the extension lines from the building to the edges of the wood block.

7. Cut out the building. You should have no difficulty doing this, since it is simpler than the Fisher-Martin House.

8. Sand and seal the edges and the back of the building.

9. Mix white and black to create a light gray color for the roof. Compare your sample with that in the color section. Adjust as necessary. Apply two coats to the edges and back.

10. Label and sign the building on the back.

Having finished this building, your skills in coloring and cutting should have grown considerably from when you began the Kutztown Depot. Next is the "Ending of Controversie" House—a building with an interesting past.

6

THE "ENDING OF CONTROVERSIE" HOUSE

The "Ending of Controversie" evokes a period of religious persecution in seventeenth-century America. Wenlocke Christison, a Quaker from Massachusetts, was beaten and driven from New England because of his beliefs. He finally found a home in Maryland, a colony that had become a haven of religious tolerance under the guidance of Lord Calvert. Christison named his land for the new-found peace and built a home there circa 1670.

The house, located in Easton, is in the English Tudor tradition, although it may also be referred to as Late Medieval. The original house contained two rooms—a hall and a parlor—and was a scaled-down approximation of an English manor house. The parlor was the "best" room as compared to the utilitarian hall. Each of the two ends of the house had a fireplace and was made of brick (see floor plan). The back and front walls were identical and were constructed with vertical boards covered with batten strips. The siding of the house is similar in construction to that of the Kutztown Depot; however, the boards are of random width.

This house is a reconstruction of the original, which was razed in 1940 because it was badly decayed. Dr. Chandlee Forman, an architect who took photographs of the building before it was demolished, built a replica in 1970. It was used as a writer's studio and architect's office until 1984, when it was donated to the Historical Society of Talbot County. The house was moved to the society's garden in 1985. The reconstruction of the house omitted the parlor and left only a large hall. Since a second fireplace was not needed, the gable end of the house opposite the fireplace was constructed of board and batten.

MAKING THE MINIATURE
Prepare for coloring the house by making two photocopies of the drawing.

Coloring the Batten Siding
1. Using crosshatching, apply cream to the entire area of the wall. Because of its small area, it is not necessary to apply the color board by board as done with both the Kutztown Depot and the parish hall.

2. Burnish over the crosshatching with the cream pencil.

3. Use cool gray 20 percent for shading under the eaves and to the right of each of the dentils.

4. Use rosy beige to shade along the right-hand side of each batten strip.

Coloring the Gable End and Chimney
The instructions that follow apply to the chimney, wall, and foundation and are similar to those given for the lawyer's office.

USE THESE COLORED PENCILS
FOR THE "ENDING OF
CONTROVERSIE" HOUSE:

- blue gray
- cloud blue
- cool gray 20%
- cool gray 70%
- cream
- French gray 20%
- French gray 70%
- imperial purple
- indigo
- jade green
- light peach
- mulberry
- orange
- peach
- rosy beige
- sky blue
- terra cotta
- Tuscan red
- white

The "Ending of Controversie" House

1. Sharpen the peach pencil, and lightly apply crosshatching over the entire area of bricks—chimney, wall, and foundation.

2. Sharpen the terra cotta pencil, and apply crosshatching over the entire area. This time, however, begin forming

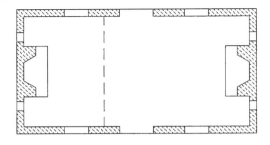

Tudor manor floor plan. *The original house had a fireplace at both ends. The reconstructed house has one fireplace and the building has been shortened to the position of the broken line.*

the individual bricks with crosshatching. Note, however, that the decorative banding on the chimney and the row of bricks paralleling the edges of the gable are not colored at this time.

3. Use Tuscan red to make the edges of the bricks more precise, stroking vertically on the ends and horizontally along the bottom edges.

4. Burnish the areas above and to the left of each brick with light, horizontal strokes, using the light peach pencil.

5. Burnish each brick with light, crosshatched strokes with the orange pencil. Use orange in parallel strokes above and below the decorative band of bricks on the chimney to further define it.

6. Use French gray 20 percent to color the decorative brick banding around the chimney and the row of bricks down each gable.

7. Use mulberry, applied very lightly with diagonal strokes, for shading on the left side of the chimney.

Coloring the Door and Window Frames

1. Use white to color the door, door frame, and window frames, following the direction of the structural members of each.

2. Apply shading to the door panels with sky blue.

3. Draw the hinges on the windows with French gray 70 percent.

Coloring the Windows

1. Use a sharp, cool gray 70 percent pencil and light, diagonal strokes to color in each windowpane.

2. Using a cloud blue pencil with a very blunt point, add shading to the upper left corners of the windowpanes.

3. Apply jade green very lightly to the shading of the windowpanes. Add a few light, diagonal strokes in other areas of the window.

4. Use the cream-colored pencil to lighten the color in the lower right-hand corners of the windowpanes.

Coloring the Roof

With this roof, as with the lawyer's office, you do not have to define the individual shingles, since they already have been drawn.

1. Apply blue gray to the entire roof area, using short, horizontal strokes. Follow with cool gray 70 percent and cool gray 20 percent with the same kind of strokes.

2. Apply jade green with short, diagonal strokes.

3. Apply indigo, very lightly, with diagonal strokes at right angles to those used in the previous step.

4. Use imperial purple with light, short, diagonal strokes to shade the area below the base and to the left of the chimney.

5. Color the roof ends of the gable with cool gray 70 percent.

When you have finished coloring the house, apply two coats of fixative to protect the surface of the drawing.

Cutting and Finishing

Instead of repeating the instructions for cutting and finishing, I will simply give you a list of steps to be followed.

1. Cut a piece of wood 4¾ inches square, and sand the back and edges.

2. Mark the corner extensions, and draw the square surrounding the house on the back of the drawing.

3. Trim the drawing; tape it to a piece of cardboard.

4. Spray adhesive on the back of the drawing, and place the wood block in position on the square.

5. Trim the excess paper from around the wood block, and rub the drawing to be sure it is well glued to the block.

6. Draw the extension lines from the building to the edges of the wood block.

7. Cut out the building with the scroll saw.

8. Sand and seal the edges and the back of the building.

9. Sand the edges and back of the house in preparation for applying sealer to the bare wood. Apply two coats of sealer, sanding after each coat has dried.

10. Mix white acrylic paint with black to make a light silver gray like that used for the Fisher-Martin House. Compare the color you mix with the color sample (see color section). Apply to the edges of the left-hand wall, roof, and right-hand gable. Put the house aside to dry. Cover your paint container so that the paint will not dry out.

11. Mix the color for the lawn, a grass green. Begin with white and add a drop each of green, blue, and yellow. Mix well and compare to the paint sample. When you are satisfied with the color of paint, and when you are sure the gray paint has dried, apply the paint to the top edges and ends of the lawn.

12. Mix the brick red for the chimney, using white, oxide red, red, and yellow. When the color appears to be correct, paint the edges and top of the chimney.

13. After the paint on all of the edges has dried, you can paint the back of the house with the light silver gray you mixed earlier. Allow to dry overnight before applying a second coat to all the edges and the back, using the same colors and following the sequence given above.

14. Label and sign the building on the back.

The skills you acquired rendering the "Ending of Controversie" House will be quite helpful for the next two buildings, which are all-brick structures.

7

ONE-ROOM SCHOOLHOUSE

One-room schoolhouses once abounded in the mid-Atlantic region. Universal education was the norm in America in the nineteenth century, and since primitive roads made transportation difficult at best, the one-room schoolhouse served many small, rural communities like Lenhartsville, Pennsylvania, where this one is located. This school replaced an earlier church school and was constructed circa 1875 shortly before the borough of Lenhartsville was incorporated in 1878. It was used as a school for eighty-two years, until 1957, when the borough became part of a consolidated school district.

All the classes in a one-room school, from first grade through junior high school and sometimes even high school, were usually taught by a single teacher, older pupils helping younger students when the teacher was otherwise occupied. Typically, a one-room schoolhouse was constructed so that both gable ends were without windows. As you entered the schoolhouse, there would be a cloakroom for the children's coats, boots, and lunch to one side of the doorway; a stove and bin for firewood or coal would occupy the area on the other side of the door. Blackboards and maps would be mounted behind the teacher's desk at the far end of the room. There would be windows along the other sides of the building. Privies were located at some distance outside the schoolhouse.

This schoolhouse does not exhibit a distinctive style of architecture in its design, although the Roman arch over the doorway might tempt us to claim it as Classical Revival. Lacking a style with which to label the building, we can best refer to it as "in the vernacular," that is, in a common, undefined style. It should be noted that the design of rural schoolhouses was a responsibility of the state's Department of Education, which furnished plans to county boards of education. The plans encompassed the latest thinking in schoolhouse design.

MAKING THE MINIATURE
As usual, you should make two photocopies of the drawing in preparation for coloring the building.

Coloring the Bricks
1. Color the area of the bricks using diagonal cross-hatching. Begin with pale vermilion, followed by poppy red.
2. Apply a widely spaced horizontal and vertical cross-hatching, using goldenrod.
3. Use terra cotta to begin drawing the individual bricks.
4. Reinforce the pattern of the bricks with Tuscan red.
5. Cover the area with random diagonal strokes of peach.
6. Burnish lightly with deco orange.
7. Use Tuscan red and blue gray to form the shadow under the gable ends.

USE THESE COLORED PENCILS FOR THE SCHOOLHOUSE:

- blue gray
- cool gray 20%
- cool gray 50%
- cool gray 70%
- deco orange
- French gray 20%
- French gray 50%
- goldenrod
- indigo
- jade green
- pale vermilion
- peach
- poppy red
- sky blue
- terra cotta
- Tuscan red
- warm gray 50%
- warm gray 70%
- white

One-room schoolhouse

Coloring the Doors, Window Frames, and Gable

1. Apply white to all surfaces of the doors, windows, frames, and gable ends. Burnish well.

2. Use French gray 20 percent to create the shadows on the door panels and the trim surrounding the fan window above the door as well as the smaller window.

3. Use French gray 20 percent to color the top edge of the gable.

Coloring the Windows

1. Apply blue gray to the top half of each windowpane.

2. Apply cool gray 50 percent in the center area of each windowpane.

3. Burnish each windowpane with white.

4. Shade in the upper portion of each windowpane with indigo.

Coloring the Bell Tower

1. Color with white all areas of the tower except that surrounding the bell.

2. Shade the cross members with jade green followed by cool gray 20 percent.

3. Darken the spaces between the balustrades with jade green and cool gray 20 percent.

4. Decorate, as shown in the color section, with small dots of terra cotta.

Coloring the Bell

1. Color the upper left side of the bell with cool gray 70 percent, pressing hard on the pencil.

2. Use jade green to color the left center of the bell.

3. Use sky blue to color the right center of the bell.

4. Add touches of each color to the rim of the bell.

5. Burnish over the whole bell very lightly with sky blue.

Coloring the Steps

1. Apply French gray 20 percent to the steps, using horizontal strokes.

2. Use warm gray 50 percent to shade the steps, concentrating the color toward each end.

Coloring the Foundation

1. Apply French gray 20 percent over the entire area of the foundation, using crosshatching.

2. Use French gray 50 percent to begin forming the shapes of the stones in the foundation. Follow with warm gray 50 percent and warm gray 70 percent.

3. Burnish to blend the colors with French gray 20 percent.

When you have finished coloring the schoolhouse, apply two coats of fixative.

Cutting and Finishing

1. Cut a piece of wood 5½ inches square, and sand the back and edges.

2. Mark the corner extensions, and draw the square surrounding the schoolhouse on the back of the drawing.

3. Trim the drawing; tape it to a piece of cardboard.

4. Spray adhesive on the back of the drawing, and place the wood block in position on the square.

5. Trim the excess paper from around the wood block, and rub the drawing to be sure it is well glued to the block.

6. Draw the extension lines from the schoolhouse to the edges of the wood block.

7. Cut out the building with the scroll saw.

8. Sand and seal the edges and the back of the building.

9. Mix white acrylic paint with black to make a light silver gray like that used for the Fisher-Martin House. Compare the color you mix to the color sample (see color section). Apply to the edges of the roof and bell tower. Put the schoolhouse aside to dry. Cover your paint container so that the paint will not dry out.

10. Mix the brick red for the edges of the walls, using white, oxide red, red, and yellow. When the color appears to be correct, paint the lower edges of the schoolhouse.

11. After the paint on all of the edges has dried, paint the back of the schoolhouse with the light silver gray you mixed earlier. Allow to dry overnight before applying a second coat to all the edges and the back, using the same colors and following the sequence given above.

12. Label and sign the building on the back.

Since you're getting so good at making bricks, I thought you should have an opportunity to do another brick building—the Adam Thoroughgood House.

8

THE ADAM THOROUGHGOOD HOUSE

This is a small plantation house that was built in Princess Anne County, Virginia, circa 1640 by Adam Thoroughgood. He was a former bond servant who worked off his passage money and rose to become a member of Virginia's House of Burgesses. The house is one of the earliest surviving brick houses built in America, if not the earliest.

The Thoroughgood House is an outstanding example of an English Tudor or Medieval hall-and-parlor house, similar in design to the "Ending of Controversie" House in chapter 6. (See the drawing in that chapter of the floor plan of the house.) The pyramidal chimney and T-shaped stacks are also Tudor in origin. Trim is of wood, painted dark brown to simulate the stone trim used with brick in Tudor England. The glazed header bricks along the gable are similar to those found in eleventh-century Normandy buildings. The windows are glazed with diamond-shaped panes that were the state of the art in glass-making of that period. American features include second-story loopholes for shooting at Indians and a secret passageway leading underground to the nearby James River, where a boat was kept waiting for emergency escapes. Today the restored Adam Thoroughgood House is owned by the Virginia Beach Historical Society and is open to visitors.

MAKING THE MINIATURE

You should not experience any difficulties in coloring this house, since there are no new techniques to learn.

Coloring the Bricks

The bricks in the Thoroughgood House are laid in a pattern known as Flemish bond. This pattern is used to tie the face row of bricks to a second row directly behind it by using a brick laid endwise between two bricks laid lengthwise. The bricks laid endwise in this house were gray instead of the more common brick red.

1. Cover the separate brick areas with diagonal crosshatching of peach, followed by pink, poppy, and goldenrod.

2. Go back over the brick areas with orange in horizontal and vertical crosshatching.

3. Using terra cotta, begin forming the bricks in long, blunt shapes, leaving a short space between each brick shape.

4. Color the spaces between the long brick shapes with French gray 50 percent.

5. Burnish overall with deco orange.

6. Touch up and further define the bricks using terra cotta, Tuscan red, and blue gray.

7. Darken the area under the eaves with imperial purple.

USE THESE COLORED PENCILS FOR THE THOROUGHGOOD HOUSE:

- blue gray
- clay rose
- cloud blue
- cool gray 20%
- cool gray 70%
- dark green
- deco orange
- French gray 20%
- French gray 50%
- goldenrod
- grass green
- imperial purple
- indigo
- jade green
- olive green
- orange
- peach
- pink
- poppy red
- straw yellow
- terra cotta
- Tuscan red
- warm gray 70%
- yellow ochre

The Adam Thoroughgood House

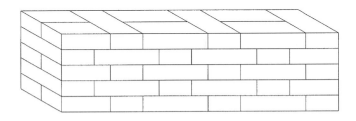

Flemish bond brick pattern. *The bricks in the Thoroughgood House are laid in a pattern known as Flemish bond. This pattern is used to tie the face row of bricks to a second row directly behind it by using a brick laid endwise between two bricks laid lengthwise.*

Coloring the Windows

1. Apply cloud blue in diagonal strokes over each glazed area of the windows.

2. Using blue gray, shade the windows with soft triangles in both the upper left and lower right corners.

Coloring the Trim and Gables

Color the gables and the window and door trim with Tuscan red. Burnish over it with blue gray.

Coloring the Door

1. Apply Tuscan red to the door with diagonal strokes, followed with a very light crosshatching of blue gray.

2. Follow the diamond pattern of the door with short strokes of warm gray 70 percent.

3. Burnish the upper point of each diamond with French gray 20 percent.

Coloring the Steps

1. Apply the blue gray to the steps in a mottled pattern—lighter in some areas, darker in others.

2. Apply random, small "splashes" of clay rose.

Coloring the Roof

1. Apply blue gray with horizontal strokes over the whole roof area. Follow with cool gray 70 percent and cool gray 20 percent, also applied with horizontal strokes.

2. Apply jade green in diagonal strokes that follow the angle of the gables. Then apply indigo in diagonal strokes at right angles to the jade green.

3. Burnish overall with cloud blue, and shade around the chimney with imperial purple.

Coloring the Lawn

1. Apply jade green in short, diagonal strokes. Follow with olive green and dark green in a crosshatch pattern.

2. Apply yellow ochre, also with crosshatching, but this time with a dull pencil point.

3. Draw in the tufts of grass with grass green.

4. Apply small areas of peach, using a horizontal stroke.

5. Apply straw yellow very lightly along the bottom edge of the lawn, using horizontal strokes.

Give the colored drawing two coats of fixative.

Cutting and Finishing

1. Cut a piece of wood 5¼ inches by 6¾ inches and sand the back and edges.

2. Mark the corner extensions, and draw the square surrounding the house on the back of the drawing.

3. Trim the drawing; tape it to a piece of cardboard.

4. Spray adhesive on the back of the drawing, and place the wood block in position on the square.

5. Trim the excess paper from around the wood block, and rub the drawing to be sure it is well glued to the block.

6. Draw the extension lines from the building to the edges of the wood block.

7. Cut out the building with the scroll saw. Note that every edge will require a closed, inside-corner cut.

8. Sand and seal the edges and the back of the building.

9. Mix white acrylic paint with black to make a light silver gray like that used for the "Ending of Controversie" House. Compare your color to the sample in the color section. Apply to the ridge and to the roof's right-hand edges.

10. Mix the color for the lawn, a grass green. Again, begin with white and add a drop each of green, blue, and yellow. Mix well and compare to the paint sample. When you are satisfied with the color of paint, and when you are sure the gray paint has dried, apply the paint to the top edges and ends of the lawn.

11. Mix the brick red for the chimney using white, oxide red, red, and yellow. When the color appears to be correct, paint the edges and tops of the chimneys as well as the right edge of the house.

12. After the paint on all of the edges has dried, paint the back of the house with the light silver gray you mixed earlier. Allow to dry overnight before applying a second coat to all the edges and the back, using the same colors and following the sequence given above.

13. Label and sign the building on the back.

To provide a little relief from brick buildings, I have selected a quaint surveyor's office for your next project.

9

SURVEYOR'S OFFICE

This surveyor's office was built circa 1870 and is now located on the grounds of the Landis Valley Farm Museum in Landis Valley, Pennsylvania. The building is Carpenter Gothic in style, as indicated by the decorative cutout "gingerbread" of the gables and the slightly arched lintels over the door and window. The gable tracery is especially attractive in the way its half-round opening echoes the form of the round window behind it.

At first glance, one would think that this surveyor's office was built as a children's playhouse, since the one-room building is only about 8 feet wide, 10 feet deep, and 10 feet high. In the nineteenth century, however, a surveyor would certainly have found sufficient space for his needs—a stove, a large desk for map drawing, and storage area for transit, chains, and other equipment.

MAKING THE MINIATURE

Though this building is simple to cut out, the complexities of its construction and painting should provide you with an interesting challenge coloring it.

Coloring the Siding

1. Begin coloring the siding by applying cobalt blue in light, horizontal strokes.

2. Follow with cloud blue, again applied with horizontal strokes.

3. The building is constructed with German siding similar to that used on the lawyer's office. This means the shadow under the lower edge of each board is concentrated in a rather narrow band. Use an ultramarine pencil with a sharp point in order to emphasize the lines of the siding.

4. For the shadow under the gable, use cobalt blue in diagonal strokes. Then apply Copenhagen blue, also using diagonal strokes.

Coloring the Door and Shutters

1. Use a cool gray 20 percent pencil to apply shadows under the steps, the panels on the shutters and door, and the frame of the lower window.

2. Apply blue slate very, very lightly to form the shadows in the door and shutter panels.

3. Blend with a coat of white.

4. Color the doorknob with yellow ochre.

Coloring the Windows

1. Color the lower window with blue gray, applying it with diagonal strokes. Repeat, this time with indigo.

2. For the green window shade as well as that in the transom, apply blue gray and then bottle green and jade green, all with diagonal strokes.

3. Reapply the blue gray, bottle green, and jade green.

4. Use horizontal strokes of blue gray for the shadows on the shades, followed with a light crosshatching of indigo in the corners.

USE THESE COLORED PENCILS FOR THE SURVEYOR'S OFFICE:

- blue gray
- blue slate
- bottle green
- cloud blue
- cobalt blue
- cool gray 20%
- Copenhagen blue
- crimson red
- deep vermilion
- French gray 20%
- indigo
- jade green
- ultramarine
- warm gray 50%
- white
- yellow ochre

Surveyor's office

5. Color the round, upper window with blue gray, followed by indigo blue along the upper left edges as shadows. Blend the indigo blue into the blue gray.

6. Apply shading to the upper window with Copenhagen blue in diagonal strokes.

Coloring the Trim and the Gable

1. Apply deep vermilion to the trim around the door, windows, and the decorative stars in the gingerbread, using smooth strokes that follow the direction of the wood.

2. Repeat using crimson red.

3. To create the shadow of the roof on the gingerbread, first use blue gray and then, for the openings in the boards, use an indigo pencil.

4. Color the upper edge of the gable with cloud blue and then blue gray.

Coloring the Steps

1. Apply French gray 20 percent to the steps, using horizontal strokes.

2. Use warm gray 50 percent to shade the steps, concentrating the color toward each end and under the overhanging treads.

When you have finished coloring the surveyor's office, apply two coats of fixative to the drawing.

Cutting and Finishing

1. Cut a piece of wood 4 inches square, and sand the back and edges.

2. Mark the corner extensions, and draw the square surrounding the surveyor's office on the back of the drawing.

3. Trim the drawing; tape it to a piece of cardboard.

4. Spray adhesive on the back of the drawing, and place the wood block in position on the square.

5. Trim the excess paper from around the wood block, and rub the drawing to be sure it is well glued to the block.

6. Draw the extension lines from the building to the edges of the wood block.

7. Cut out the building with the scroll saw.

8. Sand and seal the edges and the back of the building.

9. Mix white acrylic paint with black to make a light silver gray like that used for the Fisher-Martin House. Compare the color you mix to the color sample (see color section). Apply to the edges of the surveyor's office.

10. After the paint on all of the edges has dried, paint the back of the house with the same light silver gray. Allow to dry overnight before applying a second coat to all the edges and the back, using the same color and following the sequence given above.

11. Label and sign the building on the back.

In the next project you will have an opportunity to hone your skills in coloring siding and shutters. To make it a bit more challenging, you also will learn to color clay roof tiles.

10

MANSARD HOUSE

This house was built in Dover, Delaware, as a private home in the mid-nineteenth century and is currently owned by Wesley College, which uses it for college offices. It has a mansard roof, which is constructed in two sections: the lower section almost vertical and the upper section flat, or nearly so. This provides a higher, more useful interior. Although credited to the eighteenth-century French architect François Mansart, this type of roof was used earlier, for example, in the Louvre, a sixteenth-century building. It is characteristic of French Renaissance and, later, of European and American Victorian architecture.

Technically, the style of this house is Second Empire, named after the reign of Napoleon III, who became emperor of France in 1860. This is the term used in France to describe buildings constructed with mansard roofs during this period. However, the term is not generally used in the United States; it is common practice in this country to refer to a building with such a roof as mansard.

MAKING THE MINIATURE

Make two photocopies of the building in preparation for coloring it.

Coloring the Siding

1. Apply crosshatching of light aqua to each area of siding.
2. Burnish over with white.
3. Apply aquamarine, using a very light crosshatching.
4. Burnish with white to blend the two other colors.

Coloring the Trim, Shutters, Paneling, and Door

1. Apply an even coat of peacock blue to all dark green areas, using horizontal and vertical crosshatching. Repeat, using aquamarine.
2. Burnish over the two colors with light aqua.

3. Sharpen the indigo blue pencil, and apply shadows to the eaves.

Coloring the Red Trim, Ornaments, and Brackets

1. Apply blush pink with straight strokes, following the direction of the object being colored.
2. Repeat with pink and carmine red.
3. Burnish and blend the colors together with crimson red.

Coloring the Windows

1. Apply cool gray 20 percent to the upper left corner of each windowpane.
2. Apply cool gray 50 percent to the lower right corner of each windowpane.
3. Apply periwinkle lightly in the center area of each windowpane.
4. Burnish lightly with white in diagonal strokes.
5. Apply cool gray 50 percent very lightly over each windowpane, using diagonal strokes.

USE THESE COLORED PENCILS FOR THE MANSARD HOUSE:

- aquamarine
- blush pink
- carmine red
- cool gray 20%
- cool gray 50%
- crimson red
- French gray 50%
- indigo blue
- light aqua
- peacock blue
- periwinkle
- pink
- white

Mansard house

6. Apply just a trace of indigo blue as shadow to the upper left area of each windowpane.

Coloring the Pink Roof Tiles

Follow each step for a single, horizontal row of tiles before doing the next row.

1. Apply blush pink to each tile with horizontal strokes.
2. Apply pink to each tile with horizontal strokes.
3. Blend the two colors together with white, burnishing lightly.
4. Apply carmine red lightly in the center area of each tile.
5. Apply pink to the lower edges of each tile.

Coloring the Light Blue Tiles

1. Apply light aqua to each tile with horizontal strokes.
2. Burnish each tile with white.

Coloring the Porch Deck

1. Apply an even coat of cool gray 20 percent to the porch deck.
2. Shade the rear half of the deck with French gray 50 percent.

When you have finished coloring the mansard house, apply two coats of fixative to the drawing to protect its surface.

Cutting and Finishing

1. Cut a piece of wood 6 inches by 7 inches, and sand the back and edges.

2. Mark the corner extensions, and draw the rectangle surrounding the mansard house on the back of the drawing.

3. Trim the drawing; tape it to a piece of cardboard.

4. Spray adhesive on the back of the drawing, and place the wood block in position on the square.

5. Trim the excess paper from around the wood block, and rub the drawing to be sure it is well glued to the block.

6. Draw the extension lines from the building to the edges of the wood block.

7. Cut out the building with the scroll saw.

8. Sand and seal the edges and the back of the building.

9. Mix white acrylic paint with green and blue to make a light turquoise hue similar to the color of the siding of the mansard house. Compare the shade you mix to the color sample found in the color section. Then apply it to all the edges except the bottom edge of the house.

10. After the paint on the edges has dried, paint the back of the house with the same color.

11. Allow to dry overnight before applying a second coat to the edges and back.

12. Label and sign the building on the back.

The next building you will make is an example of an important form of commercial architecture in the nineteenth century—a general store.

Kutztown Depot. Kutztown, Pennsylvania, 1869-1870. This Victorian railroad station was built in the Gothic Revival style, also known as American Gothic and Carpenter Gothic. Characteristic features are the scalloped lower edges of the roof rafters and crossbeam, the framing of the windows and doors, and the semiarches under the eaves. The framing of the windows and doors are subtle imitations of the stonework in original Gothic buildings.

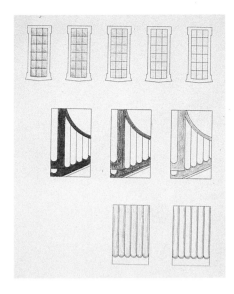

Paint color guide. Top left to right, *cream, light brown, and brick red*. Middle left to right, *light tan, light gray, and dark gray*. Bottom left to right, *turquoise and light green*. When mixing paints for the wood block, compare your color to these samples to see if your results match.

Coloring techniques. *When coloring the batten strips, trim, and windows of the Kutztown Depot, use this illustration to see how the addition of another pencil color to the previous one affects the hue.*

Fisher-Martin House. Cool Springs, Delaware, 1730 (moved to Lewes, Delaware, 1980). *Representative of the Anglo-Dutch tradition that combined English medieval houses with those of Flanders, it features a gambrel roof, with lower, steep sections and upper, flatter sections. The perspective of the miniature is from a three-quarter view. This won't be a problem when coloring the house, but take particular care when doing the roof and chimney, as their edges are different colors.*

Saint Peter's Parish Hall. Smyrna, Delaware, 1872. Similar in construction to the Kutztown Depot, this church has several Gothic features: steep gables, an arch surrounding the door, batten strips with Gothic arches under the gables, and a rose window over the door. Below, *the flecks of color serve to simulate the rose window without any actual objects being drawn.*

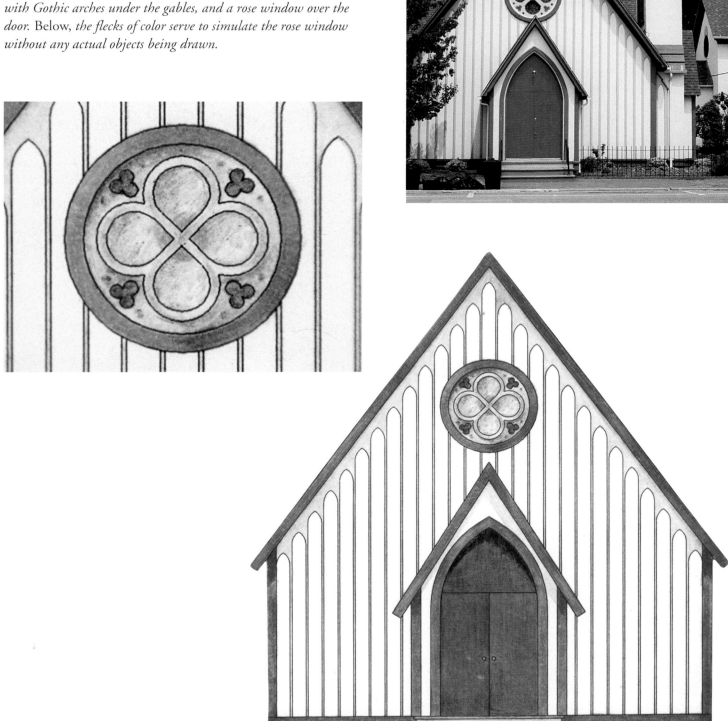

Lawyer's office. Cambridge, Maryland, c.1820. *Characteristic of the Federal style, this quaint building has a dentil beam running along the cornice, a semicircular fan light, and pilaster columns on either side of the door. Because they were inexpensive to construct and maintain, office buildings such as this were common in rural areas.*

"Ending of Controversie" House. Easton, Maryland, c. 1670. *Evoking a period of religious persecution in seventeenth-century America, this house became a haven to Wenlocke Christison, a Quaker who was beaten and banished from New England because of his beliefs. The house, built in English Tudor tradition, features a parlor, one fireplace, and batten-strip siding. Notice in the three-quarter miniature of the house that the spacing of the siding varies because of the width of the boards that were available .*

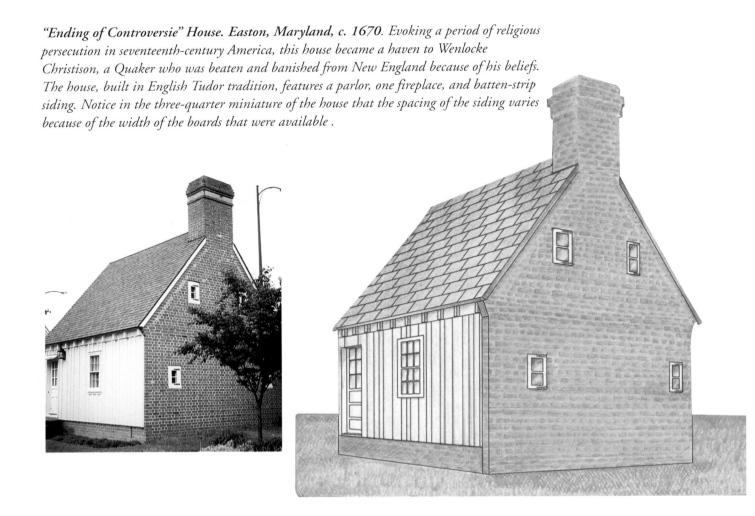

One-room schoolhouse. Lenhartsville, Pennsylvania, c. 1875. *Typical of the schoolhouses that once dotted rural America, this building does not exhibit a distinctive style of architecture but contains features of Classical Revival, such as the Roman arch over its doorway. One-room schoolhouses were designed so that both gable ends were without windows. The front wall was typically covered with blackboards and maps, and cloak closets usually ran along the back wall. Constructing windows at either end would therefore have been impractical, as well as expensive. In this schoolhouse, however, there is a window for the attic.*

Adam Thoroughgood House.
Princess Anne County, Virginia, c. 1640.
An outstanding example of English Tudor,
this house features a pyramidal chimney,
T-shaped stacks, glazed header bricks, and
windows glazed with diamond-shaped panes.
Also featured are second-story loopholes, used
for firing at attacking Indians, and a secret
passageway that leads underground to the
nearby James River.

Surveyor's office. Landis Valley, Pennsylvania, c. 1870.
Representative of the Carpenter Gothic style, this eight-by-ten foot office features a decorative "gingerbread" cut-out around the gables and slightly arched lintels over the door and window. A common decorative feature of this style is the way in which the half-round openings of the gable tracery echo the form of the window behind it.

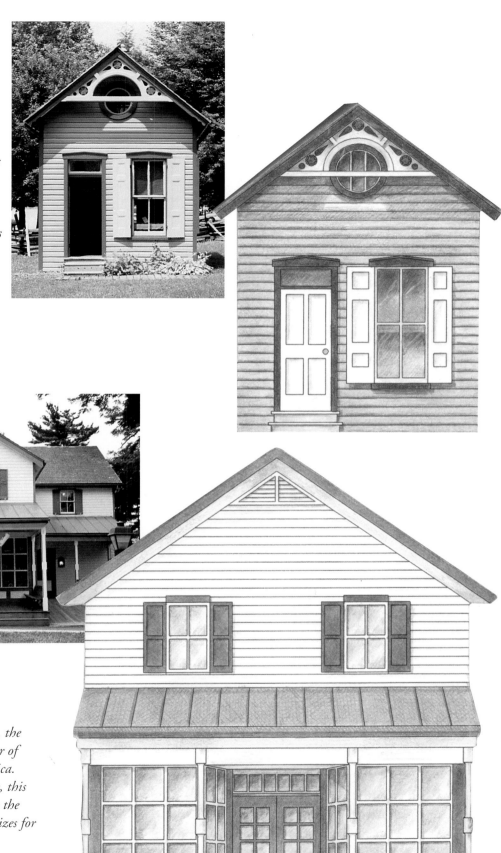

General store. Landis Valley, Pennsylvania, c. 1870.
Ranking with the church and school, the general store was an important center of activity in nineteenth-century America. Having no specific architectural style, this replica is typical of the stores built in the later part of the century when glass sizes for larger windows were available.

***Mansard house. Dover, Delaware, c. 1860*.** *Now owned by Wesley College and used for college offices, this colorful house is representative of Second Empire architecture. Characteristic of this style is the mansard roof, which was constructed in two sections: the nearly vertical lower section and the almost flat upper section. This type of roof, although credited to French architect Francois Mansart, was actually used two centuries before his time, and is characteristic of French Renaissance architecture.*

Amstel House. New Castle, Delaware, 1738. *Formerly the home of Delaware's governor Nicholas Van Dyke (1783–1786), this two-and-one-half-story brick building features a fan window and brick arches, both of which attest to its Georgian character. Further accenting this is the pent roof—the narrow, cornice-like molding that connects the eaves at both ends of the gable.*

Cape Island Presbyterian Church. Cape May, New Jersey, 1860. Classified as in the vernacular because it does not exhibit any one particular architectural style, this church alludes to Romanesque Revival with its arch-headed windows, to Classical Revival with its pilaster columns, and even to the styles of the Orient (a Victorian fascination), with the unusual onion dome on its tower. The shutters of this building reflect its seaside location and were designed to keep out both wind and rain.

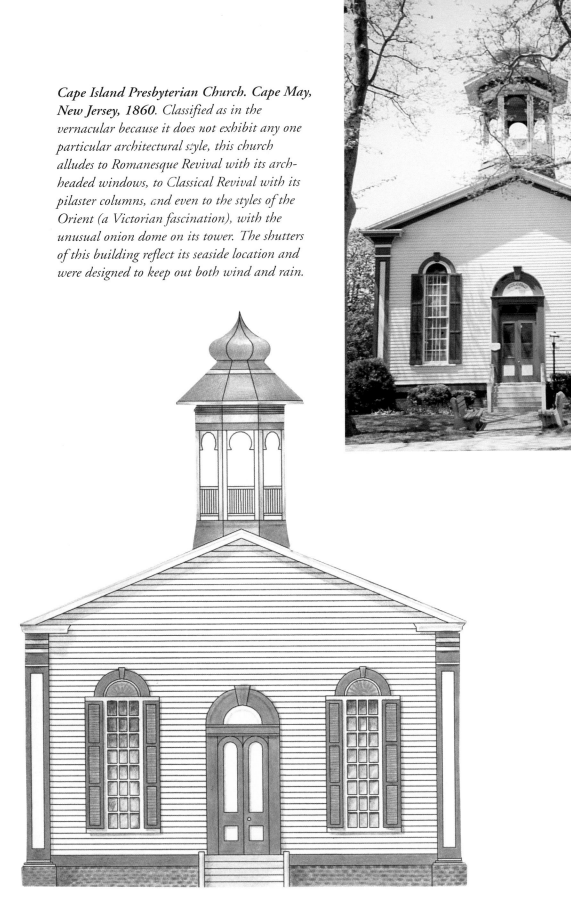

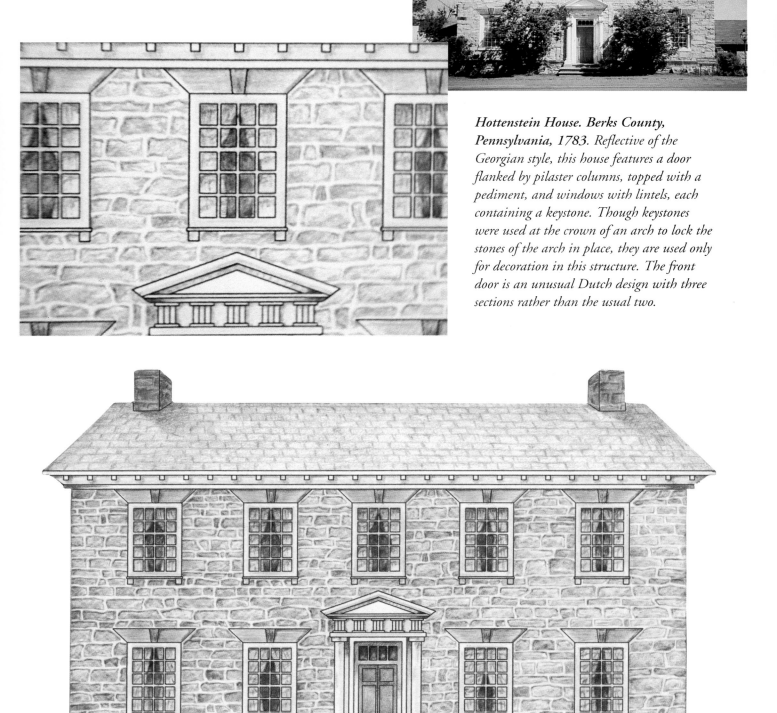

Hottenstein House. Berks County, Pennsylvania, 1783. *Reflective of the Georgian style, this house features a door flanked by pilaster columns, topped with a pediment, and windows with lintels, each containing a keystone. Though keystones were used at the crown of an arch to lock the stones of the arch in place, they are used only for decoration in this structure. The front door is an unusual Dutch design with three sections rather than the usual two.*

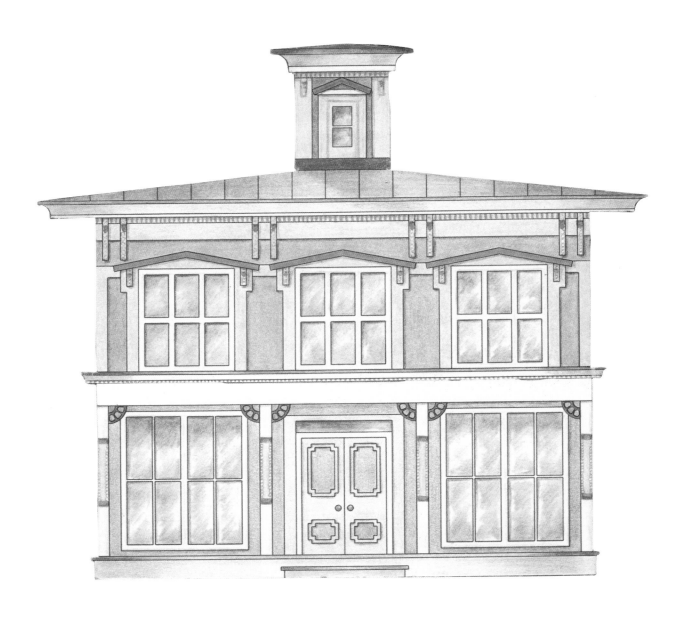

Italianate house. Milford, Pennsylvania, c. 1870. *This house is considered to be Italianate in style primarily because of the central cupola and the broad eaves. The paired windows and doors, wide structure, brackets, and stucco walls are also typical of Italianate architecture. Nineteenth-century houses with intense colors of this sort were known as painted ladies.*

New Castle Old Town Hall. New Castle, Delaware, 1823. *As architects of the early republic tried to distance themselves from the English, they borrowed from other cultures in an attempt to develop a distinctly American style. The result was the evolution of Federal architecture into what is known as Greek Revival. The town hall symbolizes the beginning of this new style with its arched entryways, hipped roof, and octagonal cupola. During its early years, this building contained the city offices and served as the fire house and federal court building.*

Cooper's Tavern. Winchester, Virginia, 1760.
This log-cabin tavern represents a style of
architecture brought to America by Swedish
colonists in 1638. During the eighteenth and
nineteenth centuries, the Scots-Irish spread this style
throughout Pennsylvania, Maryland, and Virginia.
Typical of log cabin design are its one-room
construction—Cooper's Tavern is 12 by 20 feet—
and the notching and interlocking of the logs at the
corners.

Outhouses. Known also as privies, back
houses, and thunder boxes, these buildings
did not vary greatly in design or structure.
They tended to differ only in the creative
patterns that were cut out on the door.
Symbols such as the sun, moon, and heart
were sometimes used to distinguish gender,
but their primary function was to provide
light and ventilation for the outhouse.

Pennsylvania German bank barn.
Berks County, Pennsylvania, c. 1890.
Bank barns, which farmers built into hillsides so they could drive their horses onto the second floor, were used to store farm equipment and hay and to house cattle and horses in the winter. Typical of such barns were the forebay, a large set of winnowing doors, and its hillside construction. Contrary to popular myth, the round hex signs were not used by farmers to ward off evil.

Delameter House, Rhinebeck. New York, 1844. Carpenter Gothic in style, this house features delicate ornamental barge boards, paired chimney stacks, pointed window arches, diamond-paned windows, and high-pitched gables peaked with pinnacles. During the era in which Alexander Jackson Davis built this house, colors of stone gray, slate blue, or fawn were used. Today, the house, painted in soft tan and white, remains true to this period.

11

GENERAL STORE

Next to the church and school, the general store was probably the most important community center in nineteenth-century rural America. More often than not, the post office also would be located in the general store. People would pick up their mail and pass the time of day with one another; old-timers would gather around the pot-bellied stove in the winter and sit on benches in front of the store in the summer. Children loved the stores, too, for they could find penny candies there, strategically placed at the first counter inside the door. If they had a nickel—a small fortune for a child—they could make several selections and spend deliciously long minutes on each decision. The stores sold everything from fruit, eggs, vegetables, and meats to horseshoes, parts for farm tools, shovels, nails, paint, and seeds. Whatever you needed you probably could find in a general store. With the development of supermarkets and shopping malls shortly after World War II, general stores met their demise.

A few authentic general stores can still be found in rural America. Most of these types of buildings, however, have been so remodeled and modernized that it is next to impossible to determine the form and structure of the original building. I chose this general store, even though a reconstruction, because it is a good example of this particular form of architecture. This building is located in Pennsylvania on the grounds of the Landis Valley Farm Museum, right next to the surveyor's office you made earlier. Like the surveyor's office, this building has no specific style; an architect or historian would call it vernacular. The store is typical of those built in the latter part of the nineteenth century, when glass in sizes for larger windows was more readily available. Although this store has wings that housed the shopkeeper's family, I didn't include them in the drawing since they would contribute little to the character of the store.

MAKING THE MINIATURE

Coloring the windows of this general store is its greatest challenge, since they represent almost half of the entire area of the building. Otherwise, you should experience no real difficulties. Begin by making two photocopies of the drawing.

Coloring the Posts, Window Frames, and Siding

1. Apply white to all the siding, using horizontal strokes.
2. Apply white to the window frames and porch posts, following the direction of the individual parts of each.
3. Apply light peach shading with just touches of blush pink and imperial purple.

USE THESE COLORED PENCILS FOR THE GENERAL STORE:

- aquamarine
- blue gray
- blush pink
- cloud blue
- cool gray 20%
- cool gray 50%
- dark green
- deco orange
- French gray 20%
- French gray 50%
- imperial purple
- indigo
- jade green
- light peach
- lilac
- pale vermilion
- parrot green
- peach
- periwinkle
- pink
- terra cotta
- Tuscan red
- warm gray 20%
- white

General store

Coloring the Soffit (the Area under the Gables)

1. Apply French gray 20 percent evenly the length of each soffit.

2. Shade the soffit using peach and cool gray 50 percent. Concentrate the gray near the peak.

3. Blend the colors by burnishing with white.

Coloring the Windows

1. Apply cool gray 20 percent to the individual windowpanes with diagonal strokes.

2. Apply cool gray 50 percent to the lower right side of each windowpane, using diagonal strokes.

3. Apply cloud blue lightly to the center of each pane, using back-and-forth diagonal strokes.

4. Apply jade green very lightly over the cloud blue.

5. Use imperial purple and periwinkle to make shadows in the upper left corner of each windowpane.

Coloring the Roof

The roof is made of V-crimped sheet steel painted red. The sheet metal is folded at regular intervals to form inverted Vs running the length of the sheet. This provides rigidity to keep it from bending, especially under the weight of snow. Keep this in mind as you color it.

1. Color the total roof area with pink in diagonal crosshatching. Repeat, using blush pink, peach, and terra cotta.

2. Apply pale vermilion to the roof, using horizontal and vertical crosshatching.

3. Apply Tuscan red with diagonal crosshatching to the shade areas next to the siding and along each vertical line on the roof that represents the V-crimp in the metal.

4. Blend the colors together by burnishing with deco orange.

Coloring the Trim, Gable, Rain Gutter, Shutters, and Door

1. Apply dark green to all the parts, using horizontal strokes that follow the direction of the piece being colored.

2. Apply parrot green to all parts, using diagonal crosshatching.

3. Blend the greens together by burnishing with aquamarine.

4. Apply shading with indigo, followed by blue gray and periwinkle. Apply the periwinkle with short, vertical strokes.

Coloring the Steps

1. Apply warm gray 20 percent to the edges of the treads at the top of each step.

2. Apply French gray 20 percent to the risers underneath each tread. Use a horizontal stroke, and apply evenly.

3. Use French gray 50 percent to create the shadows on the risers at each end of the steps.

4. Apply lilac very lightly to the shading.

When you have finished coloring the building, apply two coats of fixative to protect its surface.

Cutting and Finishing

1. Cut a piece of wood 5¾ inches by 6¼ inches, and sand the back and edges.

2. Mark the corner extensions, and draw the square surrounding the general store on the back of the drawing.

3. Trim the drawing of the store, and then tape it to a piece of cardboard.

4. Spray adhesive on the back of the drawing, and place the wood block in position on the square.

5. Trim the excess paper from around the wood block, and rub the drawing to be sure it is well glued to the block.

6. Draw the extension lines from the building to the edges of the wood block.

7. Cut out the building with the scroll saw.

8. Sand and seal the edges and the back of the building.

9. Mix white acrylic paint with black to make a light silver gray. Apply to the edges of the general store.

10. After the paint on all of the store's edges has dried, paint the back of the house with the same light silver gray. However, make sure you allow the paint to dry thoroughly overnight before you apply a second coat to the edges and back.

11. Label and sign the building on the back.

The next project is an historic building of the eighteenth century.

12
THE AMSTEL HOUSE

The Amstel House was constructed in New Castle, Delaware, in 1738. The two-and-a-half-story brick building has an aura of elegance and wealth befitting its history. It was the home of Delaware's governor Nicholas Van Dyke (1783–1786), and George Washington reportedly attended the wedding of Van Dyke's daughter to Chancellor Jones here in 1784.

The fan window over the front door, columns, and pediment as well as the brick arches over the first-floor windows and the central attic window all attest to the Georgian character of this building. This is further accented by the *pent roof* separating the second floor from the gable. A pent roof is the narrow, cornice-like molding that connects the eaves at both ends of the gable. Its original function was to protect the ends of timbers that supported an upper floor and projected through the walls of the building at this point. By the time this house was built, however, it was a decorative, nonfunctional structure. A brick *water table* runs between the pediment over the door and the second-floor windows. The water table serves as a kind of gutter to prevent rainwater from running over and eroding the face of the bricks below.

MAKING THE MINIATURE

The photograph of the house was taken on an early morning in spring. An automobile and a tree blocked the view, and the street was so narrow that I was unable to capture all of the house, even with a wide-angle lens. I decided to cut off the top of the gable since I could easily reconstruct that part when making the drawing.

The creation of the miniature house is straightforward and should not present any problems either in coloring or cutting out. As always, begin with two photocopies of the drawing.

Coloring the Bricks

1. Cover the entire brick area with peach, applied evenly with light, horizontal strokes. Repeat, using pale vermilion.

2. Apply sienna brown in rows of crosshatching. Repeat with goldenrod and poppy red.

3. Apply Tuscan red in a large, crosshatched pattern but with short strokes in the shadows.

4. Blend the colors together by burnishing with light peach.

5. Form the individual brick shapes with a blunt terra cotta pencil.

6. Burnish lightly with deco orange.

7. Apply rosy beige and blue gray to individual bricks selected at random.

Coloring the Trim, Door, and Shutters

1. Apply cream in long strokes, pressing fairly hard on the pencil. Follow the direction of the part being colored.

USE THESE COLORED PENCILS FOR THE AMSTEL HOUSE:

- blue gray
- cool gray 20%
- cool gray 50%
- cream
- deco orange
- goldenrod
- light peach
- pale vermilion

- peach
- periwinkle
- poppy red
- rosy beige
- sienna brown
- terra cotta
- Tuscan red
- white

The Amstel House

2. Use light peach and rosy beige for shadows and detail. Don't press hard on the pencil. You want the effect of a blurred shadow edge.

3. Blend the colors together by burnishing with the cream pencil.

Coloring the Windows

1. Apply cool gray 20 percent to the upper left corner of each windowpane.

2. Apply periwinkle softly in the center of each windowpane.

3. Apply cool gray 50 percent to the lower right corner of each windowpane.

4. Blend the colors together by burnishing with white.

When you have colored the house to your satisfaction, apply two coats of fixative to protect the surface of the drawing.

Cutting and Finishing

The Amstel House is one of the easiest to cut out. The only tricky parts are the curved sections of the cornice.

1. Cut a piece of wood 5¼ inches by 8 inches, and sand the back and edges.

2. Mark the corner extensions, and draw the rectangle surrounding the house on the back of the drawing.

3. Trim the drawing; tape it to a piece of cardboard.

4. Spray adhesive on the back of the drawing, and place the wood block in position on the rectangle.

5. Trim the excess paper from around the wood block, and rub the drawing to be sure it is well glued to the block.

6. Draw the extension lines from the building to the edges of the wood block.

7. Cut out the building with the scroll saw.

8. Sand and seal the edges and the back of the building.

9. Mix white acrylic paint with yellow and burnt sienna to make a cream color like that used for the Kutztown Depot. Compare the color you mix to the color sample (see color section). Apply to the edges of the roof and cornices.

10. Mix brick red using white, oxide red, red, and yellow. When the color appears to be correct, paint the ends of the house.

11. When the paint on the edges has dried, paint the back of the house with the cream color mixed earlier. Allow to dry overnight before applying a second coat to the edges and back, using the same colors and following the sequence given above.

12. Label and sign the building on the back.

Your next project is a building constructed over 120 years later—a church on the New Jersey coast.

13

THE CAPE ISLAND PRESBYTERIAN CHURCH

The Cape Island Presbyterian Church in Cape May, New Jersey, is a simple church with a fanciful belfry. The unusual onion dome on the tower dominates the church and echoes the Victorian fascination with styles from the Orient. The arch-headed window openings are allusions to the Romanesque style, but the pilaster columns at either side reflect the Classical Revival. Since the church doesn't express one specific style, we could refer to it as either Victorian or in the vernacular.

The shutters on the windows remind us that the church is in a seacoast town and has survived its share of storms since its construction in 1860. Today, the building serves as Cape May's Welcome Center.

MAKING THE MINIATURE
Make two photocopies of the drawing.

Coloring the Siding of the Church
1. Color the siding white with horizontal strokes, doing one board at a time.
2. Apply white to the ends of the gable and short cornice returns at either side.
3. Apply white to the panels and capitals of the pilaster columns, the frames of the windows, the panels of the doors, and the half-round panel over the door.
4. Use blue gray to create shadows under the gables and to the right sides of the left pilaster, windows, and door. Extend the shadow of the windows underneath the sills.
5. Color the bell tower using the same sequence of steps.

Coloring the Green Areas of the Church
1. Apply parrot green evenly with small, circular strokes. Repeat with grass green and dark green.
2. Apply shadows with indigo. Then blend the indigo with the other colors by burnishing with parrot green.

Coloring the Dome and Skirt on the Bell Tower
1. Apply carmine red on the lower skirt of the dome, using short, vertical strokes. Go very lightly in the central area. Repeat on the dome, but use strokes that parallel the curvature of the dome.
2. Shade the skirt and bottom of the dome, very lightly, with pale vermilion.
3. Shade the edges of the dome and skirt with poppy red. Press harder toward the outer edges, leaving a highlight slightly above the center of the dome and slightly below the center on the skirt beneath the dome.
4. Blend the colors together with deco orange, except in the highlight areas.
5. Color the band around the tower in the same sequence of steps. Then use crimson red to shade the outer ends of the band.

USE THESE COLORED PENCILS FOR THE PRESBYTERIAN CHURCH:

• blue gray	• light peach
• carmine red	• pale vermilion
• cool gray 20%	• parrot green
• cool gray 50%	• peach
• crimson red	• periwinkle
• dark green	• poppy red
• deco orange	• sienna brown
• goldenrod	• terra cotta
• grass green	• Tuscan red
• indigo	• white

The Cape Island Presbyterian Church

Coloring the Steps

1. Apply periwinkle in horizontal strokes, followed by a light application of cool gray 20 percent.

2. Blend by burnishing with white.

Coloring the Windows

1. Apply cool gray 20 percent to the upper left corner of each windowpane.

2. Apply periwinkle softly in the center of each windowpane.

3. Apply cool gray 50 percent to the lower right corner of each windowpane.

4. Blend the colors together by burnishing with white.

Coloring the Foundation

1. Cover the entire brick area with peach, applied evenly with light, horizontal strokes. Repeat, using pale vermilion.

2. Apply sienna brown in rows of crosshatching. Repeat with goldenrod, poppy red, and Tuscan red.

3. Blend the colors by burnishing with light peach.

4. Form the individual brick shapes with a blunt terra cotta pencil.

5. Burnish lightly with deco orange.

6. Form the shadows with blue gray.

When you are satisfied with the coloring of the church, apply two coats of fixative.

Cutting and Finishing

1. Cut a piece of wood 5½ inches by 6½ inches, with the grain of the wood running vertically—through the point of the dome. Sand the back and edges of the block of wood.

2. Mark the corner extensions, and draw the rectangle surrounding the church on the back of the drawing.

3. Trim the drawing; tape it to a piece of cardboard.

4. Spray adhesive on the back of the drawing, and place the wood block in position on the rectangle.

5. Trim the excess paper from around the wood block, and rub the drawing to be sure it is well glued to the block.

6. Draw the extension lines from the building to the edges of the wood block.

7. Cut out the building with the scroll saw. You will need to use closed, inside-corner cuts for the sides, roof, and bell tower. When cutting the dome, cut the edges of the skirt first, back out, and then cut from the top of the dome downward on each side to the intersection with the previous saw cut. Go slowly enough to follow the rather sharp curve of the dome.

8. Sand and seal the edges and the back of the building.

9. Mix white acrylic paint with black to make a light silver gray. Compare the color you mix to the color sample (see color section). Apply to the edge of the walls, roof, and bell tower.

10. Mix the brick red using white, oxide red, red, and yellow. When the color appears to be correct, paint the edges and top of the onion dome.

11. After the paint on all of the edges has dried, paint the back of the church with the light silver gray you mixed earlier. Allow to dry overnight before applying a second coat to all the edges and the back, using the same colors and following the sequence given above.

12. Label and sign the building on the back.

In the next project we tackle the coloring of a stone building.

14

THE HOTTENSTEIN HOUSE

The Hottenstein House was built with stone, some of which came from an earlier house on the site known to have been there in 1750. Two red sandstone plaques flanking the central second-story window and inset on the stone facade of the house bear the names of the people for whom the house was built and the year it was built: David and Catherine Hottenstein, 1783. The house is in rural Berks County, Pennsylvania. The road that the house faces, known as the Old State Road, was very important during the Revolutionary War. It ran from New England to Virginia and carried a great deal of traffic, including Hessian prisoners being taken to Reading, Pennsylvania.

The house shows a Georgian style in the design of its windows, entryway, and cornice. The door is flanked by two pilaster columns topped by a classical Greek pediment (gable). The lintels above the windows each contain a *keystone*. Keystones typically are used at the crown in arches to lock the stones of the arch in place. In this instance, however, the keystones are merely decorative, serving no structural function. The front door is an unusual Dutch door in that it has three sections rather than two. It consists of a lower half and a vertically divided upper half. The lower half, when closed, kept out farm animals; the upper half, with one section open, was just large enough to speak to visitors or to aim a gun through in the event of an attack. Story has it that the reason for such a door was not so much for protection against marauding Indians as fending off drunken men from a nearby tavern. A ballroom from the second floor was removed and is now in the Henry Francis Du Pont Winterthur Museum, where it is known as the "Fraktur" room.

MAKING THE MINIATURE

You have already encountered stonework on the foundation of the one-room schoolhouse, but this is the first building with walls that are constructed entirely of stone. The roof is also made of stone—slate tiles that are still quarried less than 30 miles from where this house stands. Making the house should prove to be a good adventure for you.

Prepare for the coloring by making two photocopies of the drawing.

Coloring the Roof

1. Apply cool gray 20 percent over the entire area of the roof. Color smoothly, using light pressure on the pencil.

2. Apply diagonal, widely spaced strokes of cloud blue.

3. Draw the slate tile with cool gray 50 percent.

4. Apply a little jade green and rosy beige in small, light areas. Apply more heavily in the shadows of the chimneys.

Coloring the Stonework

1. Apply cream to the entire area of stonework, using a diagonal crosshatching and pressing quite firmly on the

---

USE THESE COLORED PENCILS FOR THE HOTTENSTEIN HOUSE:

- black
- blue gray
- cloud blue
- cool gray 20%
- cool gray 50%
- cream
- deco orange
- French gray 20%
- French gray 50%
- French gray 70%
- imperial violet
- jade green
- light umber
- lilac
- raw sienna
- rosy beige
- sepia
- sienna brown
- warm gray 20%
- white

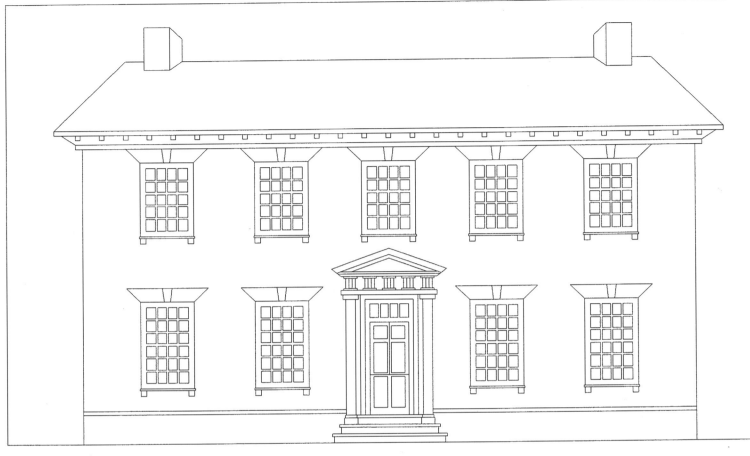

The Hottenstein House

pencil. This will form the background of the stones and also will be the color of the mortar joint separating the stones.

2. Study the way the stones are laid in building the wall and then use French gray to outline the individual stones. However, don't fill them in. Be sure to leave mortar joints around each stone. Also, since these are uncut fieldstone, strive to achieve their natural, broken shapes.

3. Use small spots of raw sienna and light umber to color the individual stones. Add rosy beige to some of the stones for variety.

4. Use French gray 70 percent to form the shadow at the top of each stone immediately below the mortar joint.

5. Using the same sequence of steps, form and color the stones of the chimneys.

Coloring the Lintels

1. In contrast to the walls, the lintels are made of cut stone. Apply cream to the entire area of each lintel using horizontal strokes. Repeat, using light umber and raw sienna.

2. Apply sepia to the keystone and also as a soft mortar shadow across the top of each lintel.

Coloring the Porch and Frames of Windows and Door

1. Apply white to all the light-colored trim on the porch, window frames, door frame, and cornice.

2. Burnish lightly over the white with cool gray 20 percent.

3. Add shading to the porch and doorway with cool gray 50 percent.

Coloring the Transom

1. Apply cool gray 50 percent to each pane in diagonal strokes, leaving a highlight in the lower center of each one.

2. Shade the top half of each pane with blue gray. Then apply black to the upper left corner of each pane.

Coloring the Door

1. Apply French gray over the door with vertical strokes, followed by French gray 50 percent with diagonal strokes.

2. Apply light umber and sienna brown in very soft streaks on the panels of the door.

3. Blend the colors together by burnishing with French gray 20 percent.

4. Use deco orange to brighten the highlights and blue gray to form the shadows.

Coloring the Windows in the Rest of the House

In coloring the windows, you will need to work very carefully to achieve the effect of curtains.

1. Apply white to each windowpane in even, diagonal strokes. Repeat, using cool gray 20 percent.

2. Apply cool gray 50 percent in the center panes to form the edges of the curtains. Darken the top of the opening with black.

3. Use some lilac and cloud blue to add a bit of color to each of the curtains.

Coloring the Steps and Water Table

The water table in the Amstel House was at the level of the second story and kept rainwater away from the bricks below. In this house, it's a stone gutter nearer to the ground, used to direct the falling rain away from the foundation.

1. Apply white with horizontal strokes to the steps and water table.

2. Use French gray 70 percent toward the ends of the steps and randomly along the water table.

3. Blend the colors together by burnishing with warm gray 20 percent.

When you have finished coloring the Hottenstein House, apply two coats of fixative to protect the drawing.

Cutting and Finishing

1. Cut a piece of wood 5 inches by 8 inches, and sand the back and edges.

2. Mark the corner extensions, and draw the rectangle surrounding the house on the back of the drawing.

3. Trim the drawing; tape it to a piece of cardboard.

4. Spray adhesive on the back of the drawing, and place the wood block in position on the rectangle.

5. Trim the excess paper from around the wood block, and rub the drawing to be sure it is well glued to the block.

6. Draw the extension lines from the building to the edges of the wood block.

7. Cut out the building with the scroll saw. The chimneys require a closed, inside-corner cut, but they are spaced far enough apart that you should be able to make nice, clean cuts. Pay close attention when cutting the cornice at the two ends of the roof, so that you preserve the stepped appearance. You should be able to cut the curve in the cornice by cutting up from the bottom edge.

8. Sand and seal the edges and the back of the building.

9. Mix white acrylic paint with black to make a light silver gray. Apply it to the edges of the roof and cornices.

10. Mix white paint with burnt umber and burnt sienna to make a light brown. Compare your mix to the color sample (see color section). When you have mixed the appropriate color, paint the edges of the two ends of the house.

11. After the paint on all of the edges has dried, paint the back of the house with the light silver gray you mixed earlier. Allow to dry overnight before applying a second coat to all the edges and the back, using the same colors and following the sequence given above.

12. Label and sign the building on the back.

Your next project, an Italianate house, presents color challenges different from those of the Hottenstein House.

15

ITALIANATE HOUSE

We had driven by this house numerous times on our way to and from New England but never really noticed it until we began this project. There it was, recently painted and a colorful sight to see. A real "Painted Lady"! Little is known about this building. It is on a main street in Milford, Pennsylvania, and probably was built shortly after the Civil War. It is called Italianate because of the cupola in the center, which is reminiscent of the campaniles (bell towers) of Northern Italy, and because of the broad eaves, also Italian in nature. Other Italianate features include the stucco walls, paired windows and doors on the first floor, wide and bracketed treatment surrounding the windows on the second floor, and heavily profiled and paired brackets supporting the eaves. Evidently, architects of this period liked things done in pairs.

MAKING THE MINIATURE

The house is relatively easy to color, but you should still begin by making two photocopies of the drawing.

USE THESE COLORED PENCILS FOR THE ITALIANATE HOUSE:

- blue gray
- carmine red
- cool gray 20%
- cool gray 50%
- cool gray 70%
- crimson red
- French gray 20%
- French gray 70%
- light peach
- metallic copper
- metallic green
- violet blue
- warm gray 20%
- warm gray 50%
- warm gray 70%
- white

Coloring the Stucco Walls

1. Apply warm gray 50 percent lightly to the stucco with vertical strokes, followed by horizontal strokes. Don't forget to do the stucco around the window in the cupola. Do the door panels at this point also, using the same color.

2. Burnish with warm gray 20 percent.

3. Trace around the panels and under the cornice on the second floor with cool gray 20 percent to give them a sense of depth.

4. Trace along the right-hand sides of the windows on the first floor and below the white porch cornice, also for depth.

Coloring the Door, Outer Door Frame, Cornice, Eaves, and Trim

1. Apply an even coat of French gray 20 percent.

2. Burnish with light peach.

Coloring the White Trim and Red Decorations

1. Apply white to the door and window frames, porch cornice, and the band across the cupola. Use crosshatching where possible; otherwise, follow the direction of each part.

2. Apply the gold decorative trim on the porch posts and the roof brackets with French gray 70 percent. Use a very sharp point to make the small circles with white centers.

3. Color the red decorations first with carmine red and then with crimson red.

Coloring the Roofs

1. Color the roof of the cupola with warm gray 70 percent. Burnish with metallic green.

2. Study the photograph of the house, and then apply warm gray to the ends and center sections of the roof.

Italianate house

3. Apply metallic green and metallic copper to the central areas of the roof. Burnish lightly with warm gray 20 percent to blend the colors.

Coloring the Porch Steps

1. Apply warm gray 20 percent lightly to the entire porch area.

2. Apply shading with warm gray 50 percent to the ends of the porch and the riser under the step.

3. Darken the edge of the porch floor and tread of the step with cool gray 50 percent.

Coloring the Windows

1. Apply cool gray 50 percent to the upper left side of each windowpane.

2. Apply blue gray to the lower right side of each windowpane.

3. Blend the two areas of color together by burnishing with white.

4. Apply cool gray 70 percent to the edges of the left corners of each windowpane.

5. With a sharp, violet blue pencil, add a little color to the upper edge of the transom window over the door.

Apply two coats of fixative to the drawing after you have finished coloring it.

Cutting and Finishing

1. Cut a piece of wood 6¼ inches by 7 inches, and sand the back and edges.

2. Mark the corner extensions, and draw the rectangle surrounding the house on the back of the drawing.

3. Trim the drawing; tape it to a piece of cardboard.

4. Spray adhesive on the back of the drawing, and place the wood block in position on the rectangle.

5. Trim the excess paper from around the wood block, and rub the drawing to be sure it is well glued to the block.

6. Draw the extension lines from the building to the edges of the wood block.

7. Cut out the building with the scroll saw. The eaves with the curved ends will be the most difficult to cut. Cut the curve after you have cut the upper and lower edges of each of the eaves.

8. Sand and seal the edges and the back of the building.

9. Mix white acrylic paint with black and raw umber to make a warm gray. Compare the color you mix to the color sample (see color section). Apply to the edges of the house.

10. After the paint on the edges has dried, paint the back of the house with the warm gray. Allow to dry overnight before applying a second coat to the edges and the back, using the same warm gray.

11. Label and sign the building on the back.

You have one more brick building to make—the New Castle Old Town Hall.

16

THE NEW CASTLE
OLD TOWN HALL

The New Castle Old Town Hall in Delaware was constructed in 1823. During its early years it contained city offices and served as the firehouse and as the federal court building. At one time there was a market house behind the town hall. Access to this market was through the central-arched passageway.

The Federal period was an era in which some architects in the United States sought to distance themselves from their English cousins by developing a distinctly American style of architecture. Borrowing from classical traditions,

this style ultimately developed into what is known as the Greek Revival (see chapter 21). We can see some of the beginnings of this architecture in the town hall with its arched entryways, *hipped roof* (one in which two sloped roofs meet one another) with balustraded deck, and octagonal cupola.

MAKING THE MINIATURE
Make two photocopies of the drawing.

Coloring the Bricks
When you are coloring the brick facade of this building, keep in mind that the building is three stories high from the ground to the eaves, a distance of some 30 feet. Most courses of bricks are about 2½ to 3 inches wide. This means that the actual building has more than 120 courses of bricks. The miniature building is only about 4 inches from base to eaves. If you attempted to draw in 120 courses of bricks, each course would be about 1/32 inch wide. Therefore, you should simply strive to suggest many courses of bricks, not the actual number. Coloring the bricks is a process of gradually creating not only the general color tone of the facade but, simultaneously, the suggestion of individual bricks. While you are coloring the bricks, try to show how the sills under the windows and the arches over the entryways are formed by bricks laid edgewise. A sharp pencil will help define the edges of the bricks. Remember all this as you work through the following steps.

1. Apply a layer of light peach to the brickwork, using light strokes and diagonal crosshatching to provide a foundation for the bricks.

2. Follow the light peach with goldenrod. Use diagonal crosshatching again, but this time form small rectangular shapes to represent individual bricks.

USE THESE COLORED PENCILS FOR THE OLD TOWN HALL:

- blue indigo
- burnt ochre
- cloud blue
- cool gray 20%
- cool gray 50%
- copper beech
- cream
- French gray 50%
- French gray 70%
- goldenrod
- indigo
- jade green
- light peach
- light umber
- light violet
- metallic copper
- orange
- peach
- poppy red
- rose pink
- sepia
- sienna brown
- terra cotta
- Tuscan red
- white
- yellow ochre
- yellowed orange

The New Castle Old Town Hall

3. Apply peach with crosshatching to further enhance the shape of the bricks.

4. Orange is applied next, but this time use both vertical and horizontal crosshatching.

5. Use yellowed orange and poppy red with diagonal crosshatching to finish forming the bricks.

6. Apply terra cotta in short, crosshatching strokes, moving away from the edges of a feature such as a window toward the center of the space between it and the next feature or an outer edge. Repeat with sienna brown. Apply Tuscan red in a large but light crosshatching over the entire brick surface.

Coloring the Roof

The original roof of the town hall was covered with wood shingles. Note in the colored drawing how the vertical edges of the shingles in the center area of the roof diverge as they move toward the outer edges. If you think you will find it difficult to achieve this gradual change of direction, you can draw in some very light lines as you did when drawing the shingles on the roof of the Fisher-Martin House. Use a straightedge along both sides of the roof to find the vanishing point, and make a very small mark with the pencil. Use this mark to help you draw the edges of the vertical shingles.

1. Apply yellow ochre in light, vertical strokes that diverge as they move away from the center. Repeat with yellow ochre, using light, horizontal strokes.

2. Apply goldenrod in diagonal crosshatching.

3. Use light umber and apply vertical strokes as you did with the yellow ochre.

4. Apply burnt sienna followed by sienna brown in thin rows to represent the bottom edges of the shingles.

5. Apply sepia followed by burnt ochre in very light, vertical strokes to define the edges of shingles in addition to the weathered pattern of the wood grain. Repeat the above steps to define the shingles further, this time using French gray 70 percent.

6. Use metallic copper in short, vertical strokes on some of the shingles toward the outer edges of the roof.

7. Use copper beech in crosshatching along the edges and under the white trim of the balustraded deck.

Coloring the Trim

1. Apply cream with short, vertical and horizontal crosshatching strokes.

2. Follow with rose pink for highlights.

3. Use yellow ochre for shading, especially around the door panels, followed by peach. Be sure to extend the base of the cupola down to the deck above the roof by applying the colors in the spaces between the balusters.

4. Burnish with white.

5. Use light violet on the outer edges of the eaves, followed with terra cotta applied very gently in the center.

Coloring the Windows

1. Apply cloud blue in diagonal strokes within the confines of each windowpane.

2. Follow with cool gray 20 percent, applied in diagonal strokes at right angles to those of cloud blue.

3. Apply jade green in soft, horizontal strokes followed by cool gray 50 percent in the upper right corners of each windowpane as shading.

4. Apply white in the opposite corners of the windowpanes. Use an eraser to soften the effects of the color in the center of each pane.

5. The shutters under the dome of the cupola can be colored with cloud blue.

6. Apply indigo in light, horizontal stripes to represent the individual slats of the shutters.

When you are satisfied with your coloring of the town hall, apply two coats of fixative to the drawing in preparation for cutting it out.

Cutting and Finishing

1. Cut a piece of wood 5 inches by 8 inches, with the grain parallel to the long side of the wood block. Sand the back and edges.

2. Mark the corner extensions, and draw the rectangle surrounding the town hall on the back of the drawing.

3. Trim the drawing; tape it to a piece of cardboard.

4. Spray adhesive on the back of the drawing, and place the wood block in position on the rectangle.

5. Trim the excess paper from around the wood block, and rub the drawing to be sure it is well glued to the block.

6. Draw the extension lines from the building to the edges of the wood block.

7. Cut out the building with the scroll saw. Study the building to see where you will have to make closed, inside-corner cuts. You probably will find the greatest difficulty in cutting the cupola and the balustraded deck beneath it.

8. Sand and seal the edges and the back of the building.

9. Mix white acrylic paint with burnt umber and burnt sienna to make a light brown like that of the color sample (see color section). Apply the paint to the edges of the town hall.

10. After the paint on the edges has dried, paint the back of the town hall with the same light brown. Allow to dry overnight before applying a second coat to all the edges and the back using the same color.

11. Label and sign the building on the back.

The old town hall is the last of the buildings constructed entirely with bricks. Now we turn to quite a different challenge—a log building.

17

COOPER'S TAVERN

Cooper's Tavern was built in the town of Winchester, Virginia, in 1760. It was recently moved to the grounds of the Winchester/Frederick County Chamber of Commerce and Visitor Center. The tavern is a very small building, about 12 feet by 20 feet. One wonders how many customers could be served in a building of this size. There is evidence, though, that the building was once joined by a second building at the center of the rear of the structure. As can be seen in the accompanying photograph, the chimney was constructed from rough fieldstone, which abounds in the area.

The origins of the log cabin are lost in prehistory, but the style of architecture was brought to America by Swedish colonists in 1638. Fort Christina, now Wilmington, Delaware, was built on the lower reaches of the Delaware River. The buildings within the fort were of log construction. During the eighteenth and nineteenth centuries, Scots-Irish settled in Delaware and then rapidly passed on to the backwoods of Pennsylvania, Maryland, and Virginia, taking with them knowledge of log cabin construction. The style is best suited to one-room buildings. The strength of this type of construction lies in the logs themselves and in the way the logs are notched and interlocked at the corners. The logs, however, are also a limitation: Their length not only determines the size of the building but also creates only one inside room. To accommodate larger families, a second floor directly above the first might be constructed, or two separate log cabins might be built and joined by a roofed porch that also could serve as an entryway.

MAKING THE MINIATURE
Make two photocopies of the drawing.

Coloring the Logs
The log cabin was a difficult building to draw on my computer, since the computer's drafting program works in terms of geometric shapes: circles, squares, and straight lines. There are almost none of these shapes in the log cabin.

1. Apply dark brown lightly to the sides of the logs but more heavily on their cut ends.

2. Use raw sienna to create splotchy yellowish areas on the log where the sun has bleached them.

3. Use dark umber with diagonal strokes to create the shadow under the eaves.

4. Use sienna brown to create the reddish areas on the logs.

5. Use French gray 50 percent to create the grayish areas on the logs.

6. Apply short, vertical marks on the logs with dark brown to simulate ax marks.

7. Apply warm gray 70 percent as shadows along the bottom edges of the logs.

USE THESE COLORED PENCILS FOR COOPER'S TAVERN:

- blue gray
- carmine red
- cool gray 20%
- cool gray 50%
- cream
- dark brown
- dark green
- dark umber
- French gray 20%
- French gray 50%
- jade green
- olive green
- straw yellow
- periwinkle
- raw sienna
- rosy beige
- sienna brown
- straw yellow
- Tuscan red
- warm gray 70%
- white

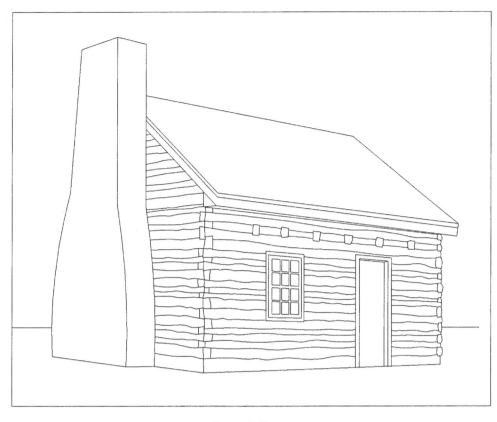

Cooper's Tavern

Coloring the Mortar

1. Apply white evenly to the mortar areas, using horizontal strokes.

2. Add cream to the mortar areas, also using horizontal strokes.

3. Use French gray 50 percent to create the shadows of the logs on the mortar.

4. Blend the colors together by burnishing lightly with cream.

Coloring the Door, Door Frame, and Window Frame

1. Apply sienna brown lightly to all parts of the door, door frame, and window frame.

2. Apply dark brown to create the shadowed areas on the two frames.

3. Use raw sienna to create the highlights on the door and parts of the frames.

4. Blend the colors together by burnishing lightly with sienna brown.

5. Create the streaks in the door with French gray 50 percent.

6. Darken the shadows in the corners of the frames with dark umber.

Coloring the Roof

1. Apply spaced, horizontal lines of cool gray 20 percent to represent the ends of the rows of shingles.

2. Apply rosy beige very lightly with crosshatching over the entire roof area.

3. Use French gray 50 percent to mark out the individual shingles. Follow with warm gray 70 percent, but apply it in different places.

4. Add short, vertical strokes of rosy beige to the individual shingles.

5. Blend the colors together by burnishing with cool gray 20 percent. Burnish harder in some areas than in others in order to give a somewhat streaky appearance to the roof.

Coloring the Window

1. Apply cool gray 20 percent to the upper left corner of each windowpane.

2. Apply cool gray 50 percent to the lower right corner of each windowpane.

3. Apply just a touch of periwinkle to the center area of each windowpane.

4. Blend the colors together by burnishing lightly with white.

Coloring the Chimney

Coloring the stones in the chimney of the log cabin follows the sequence you used on the Hottenstein House, but in this case, the mortar joint between the stones is not nearly so pronounced.

1. Apply cool gray 20 percent with a blunt point to create a mottled effect—darker in some areas, lighter in others.

2. Apply French gray 50 percent in small spots and thin lines to simulate mortar between the stones. Repeat, using French gray 20 percent.

3. Use blue gray to form darker areas and shadows. Use lightly over the left half of the chimney so that it will appear to be getting less sunlight than the right half.

Coloring the Lawn

1. Apply jade green in a crosshatch pattern, using short, curved strokes. Repeat, using olive green.

2. Use dark green near the edge of the cabin and to draw the stems of the flowers.

3. Blend the colors very lightly, using straw yellow with horizontal strokes.

4. To represent flower blossoms, put in dots of color with carmine red and Tuscan red.

When you have finished coloring the log cabin, give it two coats of fixative.

Cutting and Finishing

1. Cut a piece of wood 4¼ inches by 5 inches, and sand the back and edges.

2. Mark the corner extensions, and draw the rectangle surrounding the cabin on the back of the drawing.

3. Trim the drawing; tape it to a piece of cardboard.

4. Spray adhesive on the back of the drawing, and place the wood block in position on the rectangle.

5. Trim the excess paper from around the wood block, and rub the drawing to be sure it is well glued to the block.

6. Draw the extension lines from the building to the edges of the wood block.

7. Cut out the building with the scroll saw. When you cut out the right end of the cabin, use a wavy line to simulate the edges of the logs.

8. Sand and seal the edges and the back of the building.

9. Mix white paint with raw umber and black to make a light brown. Apply it to the two edges of the roof

10. Mix the color for the lawn—a grass green. Again, begin with white and add green, blue, and yellow. Apply the paint to the top edges and ends of the lawn.

11. Mix white paint with black to make a light silver gray, and apply it to the edges and top of the chimney.

12. After the paint on all of the edges has dried, paint the back of the house with the light silver gray. Allow to dry overnight before applying a second coat to all the edges and the back, using the same colors.

13. Label and sign the building on the back.

To add an even more rural flavor to your village, the next project you will work on is a Pennsylvania German bank barn.

18
PENNSYLVANIA GERMAN
BANK BARN

The Pennsylvania German bank barn, or forebay barn, originated in Europe. The barns are found there today, especially in south Germany, Switzerland, and Austria. In fact, the barn is frequently referred to as a Sweitzer barn, indicating its origins. The miniature bank barn in this chapter is based upon the barn shown in the photograph, which was built about 1890 in Berks County, Pennsylvania.

Barns, like covered bridges, tend not to be defined by a specific architectural style. Rather, they are categorized according to their manner of construction and their intended use. Tobacco barns are quite different from horse barns, and horse barns are quite different from bank barns. The bank barn was built to be used for general farming purposes—to store farm equipment, to house cattle and horses in the winter, and to store hay needed to feed the animals from one growing season to the next. As a consequence, the bank barn consisted of a ground floor, reserved for housing animals, and one or more upper floors for storing hay, commonly referred to as hay mows. The barn was usually two but sometimes three or more stories high.

The bank barn has several unique features. The first is the forebay, an extension of the second floor over the first providing outdoor shelter for the farmer doing his chores and for the animals in bad weather. A second feature, and why the barn is called a "bank" barn, is that it was built into the side of a hill, if possible, so that the farmer could drive into the barn on the second floor with a team of horses and a wagon full of hay or grain. If a hill was not available, a ramp would be built to the second-floor doors on the back of the barn. The third feature of the bank barn is the set of large doors on the second floor facing out over the forebay. These doors, much too high for loading and unloading materials from the ground, or for that matter from the bed of a wagon, are *winnowing* doors that served to direct wind into the barn to blow away the chaff when

grain was being winnowed. This process is an interesting one. Bundles of grain were placed on the floor, and the farmer and his helpers would beat the grain with flails to free the grain from the stalks. The flooring was laid with tight-fitting boards so that grain would not slip through. The stalks—or straw—would then be removed and stored for other uses, and the grain on the floor would be swept into a pile. The grain would be shoveled into a winnowing basket and then poured from shoulder height in a steady stream onto the floor. The wind coming in through the open doors would blow the chaff away, and the grain would be clean.

With the development of silos for storing hay and grain and the combine for threshing grain, the large forebay barn was no longer needed. And though many of them still exist, new ones are seldom built because of changing agricultural practices.

MAKING THE MINIATURE

Although modeled after the barn in Berks County, the miniature has certain different features. In making this particular miniature, I made a composite drawing of the barn with those features I felt were typical of the Pennsylvania German barn. The miniature I designed has round hex signs, whereas the original doesn't. It has arches over the winnowing doors, whereas the Berks County one doesn't. And the original has windows over two of the winnowing doors, but the miniature doesn't.

This barn is probably the most complicated building to color because of its many different features.

Coloring the Siding and Doors

1. Color the siding and the barn doors with warm gray 50 percent, using vertical strokes. Repeat, again using vertical strokes, with crimson red.

2. Apply Tuscan red with large crosshatching in very

light strokes. Follow with blue gray applied with rather widely spaced vertical strokes.

3. Apply madder carmine in a crosshatch pattern, again somewhat widely spaced.

4. Finish by using dark violet to apply shading under the eaves and the forebay.

Coloring the Hinges

Using a very sharp pencil, apply Tuscan red fairly heavily to the hinges, followed by a burnishing coat of warm gray 70 percent.

Coloring the Dark Trim

Apply Tuscan red to the dark trim of the barn as well as the crossbracing of the upper half of the opened Dutch door and the grillwork in the ventilation window next to it.

Coloring the Light Trim and Roof

1. Use a straw yellow pencil to color the roof, using a crosshatch pattern. Apply the same color to the light trim around the winnowing doors.

2. Burnish over the yellow with white.

Coloring the Hex Signs

Contrary to popular mythology, hex signs were not intended to keep evil spirits away from the barn. They were used for purely decorative purposes or, as the Pennsylvanian Germans would say, "just for pretty." Most of the hex sign designs can be made with only a compass and straightedge.

Because of the small size of the designs, you need to keep your pencils very sharp. You also probably will want to rotate the paper as you work in order to fill in the details of the hex sign more easily.

1. Start with the star. Apply crimson red to half of each point. Begin at one point and work your way around the star; be careful you don't color the wrong half of a point. Repeat with the other stars. Resharpen your pencil frequently.

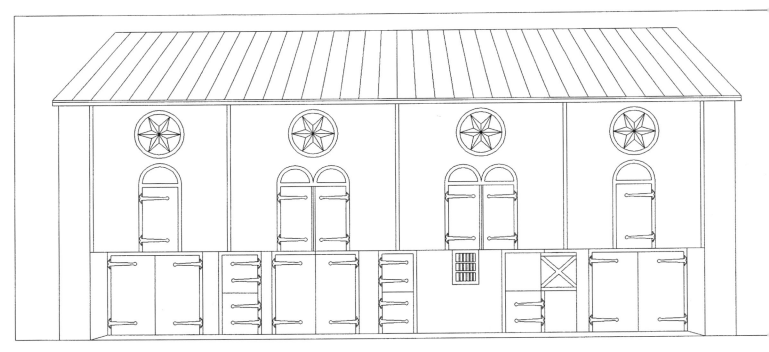

Pennsylvania German bank barn

2. Use delft blue to color the other half of each point of each star.

3. Use a deep cadmium pencil to fill in the area between the stars and the inner edge of the surrounding circle.

4. Finally, use delft blue again to color the circular band of the hex sign.

Coloring the Stonework

The stonework probably presents the greatest challenge because of the subtle differences between individual stones and the mortar surrounding them. You'll want to draw each stone in turn, sizing them appropriately to the space provided. However, in drawing a stone, let it develop its final form slowly as you place one color upon another. This will aid in conveying the soft quality of the limestone walls. Each stone in the walls needs to be defined.

1. Begin with French gray 20 percent, applying a light, overall color to the walls. You should use primarily horizontal strokes and press a bit harder in some places to begin the definition of the stonework.

2. Apply French gray 50 percent to form the edges of the stones.

3. Apply blue gray to develop corners of the stones by shading undercuts in the mortar surrounding them on their upper sides.

4. Apply warm gray 50 percent to form the shadows on the lower sides of the stones.

5. Use blue gray to delineate the edges of some, but not all, stones.

6. Darken some of the shadows with warm gray 70 percent. Then blend the whole wall with French gray 20 percent.

Sarah Grant colored this barn for me. She has a great interest in horses, but didn't tell me how you should proceed to draw and color the one in this barn. I'll have to leave you to your own devices. I am confident you can do it.

Don't forget to give your finished drawing two coats of fixative.

Cutting and Finishing

1. Cut a piece of wood 3½ inches by 8 inches, and sand the back and edges.

2. Mark the corner extensions, and draw the rectangle surrounding the barn on the back of the drawing.

3. Trim the drawing; tape it to a piece of cardboard.

4. Spray adhesive on the back of the drawing, and place the wood block in position on the rectangle.

5. Trim the excess paper from around the wood block, and rub the drawing to be sure it is well glued to the block.

6. Draw the extension lines from the building to the edges of the wood block.

7. Cut out the building with the scroll saw.

8. Sand and seal the edges and the back of the building.

9. Mix white acrylic paint with black to make light silver gray. Paint the edges of the barn.

10. After the paint on the edges has dried, paint the back of the barn also with light silver gray. Allow to dry before applying a second coat to all the edges and the back.

11. Label and sign the building on the back.

The coloring of the barn was a bit complicated, but the skills you acquired doing the earlier projects should have aided you considerably. You will be using the same skills in the next project, a "gingerbread" house.

19

THE DELAMETER HOUSE

The Delameter House was built in Rhinebeck, New York, in 1844. It is Carpenter Gothic in style. Such buildings were made possible by the invention of the scroll saw, which could cut the intricate tracery that gave these buildings the name of "gingerbread" houses. The distinguishing features of this style and of the house are the delicate ornamental *barge boards* (the gingerbread) decorating the gable, the paired chimney stacks, the pointed window arches, the diamond-paned windows, and the high-pitched gables at the peak of which are *pinnacles* (slender, decorative spars of wood extending above and below the peak and sometimes called *finials*). The roof is sheet metal painted with red lead, a color we met earlier in relation to the general store.

During the period in which this house was built, muted colors of stone gray, slate blue, or fawn were used. Its present colors are true to that era—a soft tan (fawn) and white. A modern trend in decorating gingerbread

houses is to paint them in pale blues and pink with contrasting trim in white; they are then known as "painted ladies."

The Delameter House was designed by Alexander Jackson Davis. He built it for Henry Delameter, the founder of Rhinebeck's First National Bank. The house is one of the few American Gothic residences designed by Davis that are still in existence. The house is now owned by the Beekman Arms, a local hotel, and is used to house guests.

MAKING THE MINIATURE
Make two photocopies of the drawing of the house.

Coloring the Batten Strip Siding
1. Apply French gray 20 percent in vertical strokes to the inside edges of the batten strips. Use the same color to create the shadows under the eaves.
2. Apply white to the spaces between the batten strips, blending in the French gray at the same time by burnishing.

Coloring the Trim
1. Apply rosy beige lightly to all of the trim, including the decorative gingerbread.
2. Apply French gray 20 percent lightly to the trim.
3. Mark out the details with French gray 50 percent.
4. Blend the colors together by burnishing with white.
5. Darken those trim areas in shadow with French gray 50 percent and French gray 70 percent.
6. Add French gray 70 percent to the dark trim around the door.

Coloring the Porch
1. Apply French gray 50 percent to the cornice of the porch, to the steps, and to the foundation on either side of the steps.

USE THESE COLORED PENCILS FOR THE DELAMETER HOUSE:

- carmine red
- cloud blue
- cool gray 20%
- cool gray 50%
- deco orange
- French gray 20%
- French gray 50%
- French gray 70%
- goldenrod

- jade green
- pale vermilion
- peach
- poppy red
- rosy beige
- terra cotta
- Tuscan red
- warm gray 70%
- white

The Delameter House

2. Shade the outer ends of the cornice, steps, and foundation with French gray 70 percent.

3. Blend the colors together by burnishing with white.

4. Create shadows under the edge of the floor of the porch and the treads of the steps with French gray 70 percent.

5. Burnish again with white.

6. Touch up as necessary with French gray 70 percent.

Coloring the Windows

1. Apply cloud blue with diagonal strokes to each pane of the windows and doors.

2. Apply cool gray 50 percent with vertical strokes to the lower half and left edge of each pane.

3. Add jade green with vertical strokes to some of the panes.

4. Burnish over the whole area of each window with white.

5. Darken the area between the curtains in the windows with cool gray 20 percent and cool gray 50 percent.

Coloring the Roof

1. Apply carmine red with crosshatching to each of the three areas of the roof.

2. Apply poppy red to the same areas, again using crosshatching.

3. Blend the colors together by burnishing with white.

4. Add shadows along the front edge of the upper roof with carmine red.

Coloring the Chimneys

1. Apply peach with crosshatching to the entire area of both chimneys.

2. Apply goldenrod with crosshatching to the brick area of each chimney.

3. Apply pale vermilion with crosshatching to the brick area.

4. Create brick shapes with terra cotta. Also use terra cotta to darken the alternate rows of bricks.

5. Blend the colors together by burnishing lightly with peach.

6. Further define the bricks with Tuscan red.

7. Shade the left edges of the upper chimney pipes with deco orange.

After you have finished coloring the house, apply two coats of fixative.

Cutting and Finishing

1. Cut a piece of wood 5¾ inches by 7¼ inches. Because of the extended pinnacle and chimneys, it is necessary to cut this building from a piece of wood in which the grain is vertical to the base. Otherwise, these projections would be broken off easily. As it is, the gutters and eaves at both ends of the roof are at risk, but there is really no better way to accommodate the construction of the building.

2. Mark the corner extensions, and draw the rectangle surrounding the house on the back of the drawing.

3. Trim the drawing; tape it to a piece of cardboard.

4. Spray adhesive on the back of the drawing, and place the wood block in position on the rectangle.

5. Trim the excess paper from around the wood block, and rub the drawing to be sure it is well glued to the block.

6. Draw the extension lines from the building to the edges of the wood block.

7. Cut out the building with the scroll saw. The building should be relatively simple to cut, with closed, inside-corner cuts required only for the chimneys and gable. Do not cut out the area between the two pipes extending above the brick base of the chimneys; even if you were successful, you would find it extremely difficult to paint the edges inside the openings. The pinnacle itself is rather complex, and I do not attempt to cut the saw-toothed indentations. Rather, I cut this portion of the pinnacle as a straight line and use color to indicate the indentations.

8. Sand and seal the edges and the back of the building.

9. Mix white acrylic paint with burnt umber and burnt sienna to make a light brown like that shown on the color sample (see color section). Apply the paint to the edges of the house.

10. After the paint on the edges has dried, paint the back of the house with the same paint. Allow to dry before applying a second coat.

12. Label and sign the building on the back.

With this project we come to a turning point in our miniature adventure. It's time for you to make the decisions about how to color, cut, and finish a specific building.

American Gothic house. *This drawing is offered as a challenge. Both the coloring and the cutting are left to your discretion.*

20

AMERICAN GOTHIC CHALLENGE

We were driving through northern Delaware photographing buildings for this book when we came to a crossroads marked "Odessa" and a sign pointing to the "Historic District." We didn't have any notes on houses in Odessa, but we decided to explore it anyway. There were a number of lovely buildings in the town, including the one pictured in the drawing. It was built in 1858 and is American Gothic in style. It features fancy chimneys reminiscent of those on the Delameter House, ornate brackets both under the eaves and on the porch posts, and an entryway flanked by pilaster columns. The shutters on the windows of the upper floors appear to be recent additions, whereas those on the first floor appear to be part of the original construction. The two shutters on the gable windows were installed backward and can't possibly close properly. In all probability there never were shutters on those windows. Also, in the original, one of the windows on the first floor does not have shutters. In the drawing, I removed the gable shutters and added the missing ones on the first floor.

MAKING THE MINIATURE

You are on your own with this building. I have deliberately decided to let you determine how it should be colored. The original is painted white with dark green shutters. You may want to use this scheme when you color the drawing, or you might prefer to turn it into a "painted lady," coloring it light pink and white or pale blue and white with bright red decorations similar to those on the Italianate house. The choice is yours. You also have to decide how the building should be cut and finished. Have fun!

21
DRAWING YOUR OWN BUILDINGS

If you made the buildings drawn on the previous pages, you should have acquired considerable skill in coloring, cutting, and finishing miniature wooden buildings. In this chapter I turn to the task of helping you learn to draw your own buildings so that you can make miniature buildings to document the historic structures in your community as well as the homes and businesses of friends and clients.

As so often has been the case in this project, I ran into unanticipated difficulties translating a photograph into a drawing because of untested assumptions I had made. I assumed that one could simply enlarge a photograph on a photocopying machine and, using a straightedge and drafting pen, copy the outline of the building onto a transparent mylar tracing film. When I endeavored to do this, I found several obstacles. First, enlarging the building to a size that I could accurately trace led to such blurring of detail that I was unable to determine where some portions of the structure began and ended. Consequently, those parts of the building became confused in the drawing. Second, the perspective introduced in the photograph by the position from which the picture was taken led to an awkward appearance of the building. End walls on tall buildings, for example, slanted inward toward the upper edges. Finally, even the smallest pen point I used was not up to the task of drawing such fine details of a building as window mullions (the strips dividing the panes in each window). I concluded that this was not a practical way to approach drawing miniature buildings.

At this point you probably are wondering how I managed to draw the buildings in this book. The answer is, instead of the T square, triangle, drawing board, and drafting table, I used the computer and a CAD program. CAD is an acronym for **C**omputer **A**ssisted **D**esign. It was developed for making precise engineering drawings in industries ranging from aerospace to computer chip design. By using a CAD program I can easily control scale, draw the finest detail, and correct problems of perspective. The computer is a very forgiving machine—most of the time. The only additional tool I need is a 6-inch metal rule that marks tenths of an inch. I use one manufactured by the L. S. Starrett Co. (catalog No. C305R), obtainable from most industrial supply companies.

The CAD program I use is AutoCad LT, published by Autodesk. It is an expensive program with many features that are not needed for drawing buildings. (I use it for other, more complicated projects, such as drawing gears for wooden clocks.) Quite inexpensive CAD programs will do the task just as well, if not as easily. Ask for advice at your local computer store. When you have read my description of the steps necessary to make a drawing of a building, you will be better prepared to ask pertinent questions.

You do not need a computer and CAD program to draw buildings. You can use a ruler, straightedge, compass, and pencil and make the drawing on paper. After you have finished your drawing, you can copy it onto mylar tracing film using a drawing pen. If you decide to follow this route, avoid the problems I ran into by making the drawing three times larger than the photograph. Simply multiply any measurement by three. You will find it convenient to use common fractions in your measurements rather than the tenths of an inch I use with the computer. After you have finished the drawing, you can reduce it to the desired size on a photocopying machine.

Success in drawing a building lies in having a good photograph, preferably in color. When you photograph a building, you should strive for a point of view that shows the building to its greatest advantage both structurally and aesthetically. If you want to make the building in a two-dimensional frontal view, then you should position yourself so that you are standing squarely in front of the middle of the facade. Many buildings are symmetrical with an entryway in the center. If this is the case, stand in front of the door and frame the building in the viewfinder so that it extends equally on both sides. Be careful that you are not holding the camera at an angle to the front of the building. The picture plane of the film and the front of the building should be parallel with one another.

Frame the building in the viewfinder as large as possible, but be sure you get the entire building in the photograph. There is nothing more frustrating than finding that you have cut off part of the building. You should also photograph details of the building, to be used as guides in drawing.

Sometimes you can find a good photograph on a postcard. As a matter of fact, I drew the Delameter House featured in chapter 19 from a postcard. The color photograph of it was made after the drawing was completed and served primarily to guide the coloring of the building.

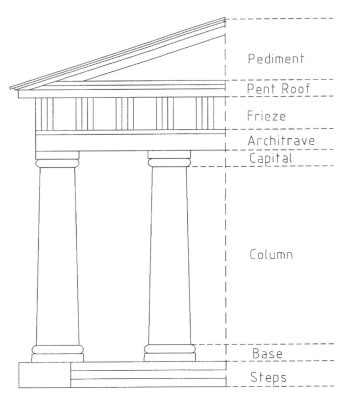

Architectural terminology. Certain technical terms are necessary when talking about a Classical Revival building. This drawing shows the terminology for various parts of the bank.

DRAWING BY COMPUTER: THE EXCHANGE BUILDING IN 13 STEPS

The building I am going to use for the demonstration drawing is the Exchange Building built in Petersburg, Virginia, in 1839. Although originally a bank, it now houses the Siege Museum. It's a good example of the Classical Revival style of architecture, which was a return to the architectural styles of ancient Greece and Rome. Thomas Jefferson was an early proponent of the Classical Revival. His home, Monticello, as well as many of the federal buildings in Washington, D.C., are built in this style. Notice in the photograph that the main entrance to the building is at the top of a stairway of some fifteen steps, reminiscent of the Parthenon atop the Acropolis in Greece.

In order to demonstrate how to draw a building using the computer, I have broken the task into steps that relate to specific architectural details, such as a pediment, column, or window. There is a drawing associated with each step so that you can see how the lines I draw on the computer screen result finally in a recognizable drawing of the building.

Step 1. In this step I draw a rectangle.

The photograph of the bank measures 3½ inches by 5 inches. Therefore, after starting the CAD program, the first thing I do is draw a rectangle on the screen the same size as the photograph—3½ inches by 5 inches. (If you were drawing the building with pencil and paper, you would make the rectangle 10½ inches by 15 inches—three times the size of the photograph.) Notice that the rectangle is drawn with a broken line. In the next step, the rectangle will become a solid line and the lines drawn in that step will be broken. Therefore, you can immediately tell at any step the part of the building that is being drawn.

Step 2. In this step I outline the *colonnade* of the Exchange Building. I have made five separate drawings so you can see how each line contributes to the drawing.

I measure from the left edge of the photograph to the peak of the pediment and then draw a line "offset" from the left edge of the rectangle on the computer. Offset, in CAD language, means to draw a line parallel to another at a specific distance. So in this instance, I draw a line on the computer parallel to and 2½ inches to the right of the rectangle's left edge. This line becomes the centerline of the

Exchange Building. *This bank in the Classical Revival style was built in 1839 in Petersburg, Virginia. Currently, it houses the Siege Museum.*

Step 1. *The outline of the photograph of the bank is drawn to actual size.*

drawing; many measurements are made from it. Then I measure from the bottom edge of the photograph to the bottom of the pediment and the peak of the pediment and draw two equivalent lines on the computer. Next, I measure the distances on the photograph and draw two more lines, one to the left, the other to the right of the centerline to indicate the ends of the pediment. Then I measure from the bottom edge of the photograph to the base of the columns and draw the equivalent line on the computer. Finally, I draw the two lines forming the pediment's gable.

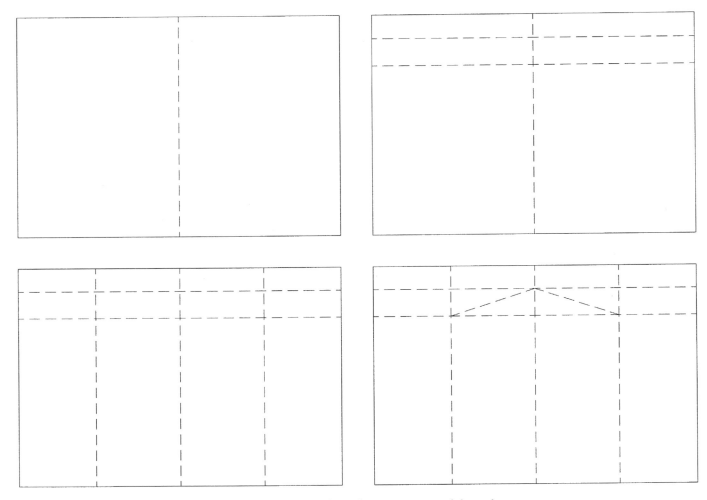

Step 2a. *Four drawings show the construction of the pediment.*

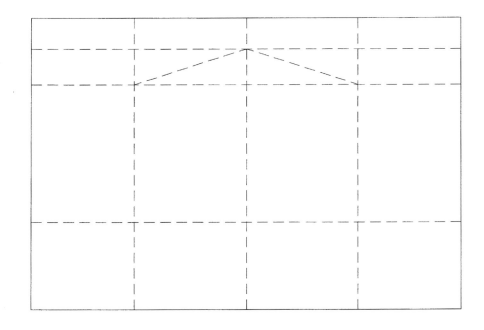

Step 2b. *This drawing defines the outer edges of the colonnade.*

Step 3. In this step I define the area between the pediment and the top of the columns—the *frieze* and *architrave*. I also draw the left and right ends of the main body of the building. I will use five separate drawings to show you how every additional line contributes to the task.

I measure in from the left and right edges of the photograph to the left and right edges of the main body of the building and draw these lines. I measure from the bottom of the photograph to the top of the frieze and draw this line connecting the two outer ends of the building. I measure the width of the frieze on the photograph and draw its bottom line. Then I measure the width of the architrave and draw its bottom line. Finally, I measure

from the edge of the photograph to the outer edge of the frieze and architrave and draw these lines parallel to the outer ends of the building.

Step 4. In this step I draw the *dentils*. I will use two drawings to demonstrate this step.

First, I trim the two lines forming the ends of the pediment, leaving just a short length of eaves. Then I measure the width of the individual dentils and the width of the spaces between the dentils, count the number of dentils and spaces, and divide the frieze into the same widths. After drawing the dentils, I draw two lines dividing each dentil into three spaces.

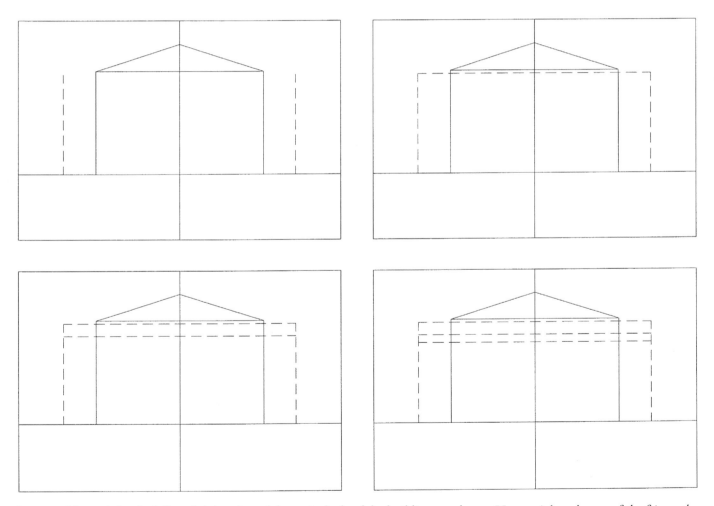

Step 3a. Upper left, *the left and right edges of the main body of the building are drawn.* Upper right, *the top of the frieze, the line connecting the two outer ends of the building, is drawn.* Lower left, *the bottom lines of the frieze are drawn.* Lower right, *the bottom line of the architrave is drawn.*

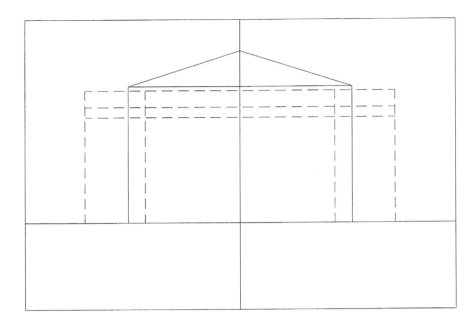

Step 3b. *The area between the pediment and the top of the columns is defined, and the left and right ends of the main body of the building are drawn.*

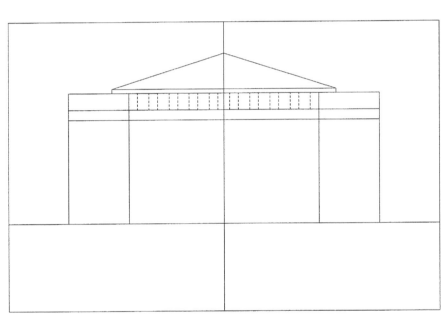

Step 4a. *The frieze is divided between the dentils and the spaces between the dentils.*

Step 5. In this step I further define the pediment. I will use five drawings to demonstrate this step.

I measure the width of the first line of molding on the gables and draw these two lines. I measure the width of second line of molding on the pent roof and draw this. I measure the third line of molding on the gables and draw this. I measure the width of the eaves on the main part of the building and draw them. Finally, I measure the distance from the edge of the photograph to the ends of the pent roof and draw a vertical line at each end.

Step 6. In this step I further refine the pediment and frieze by drawing the narrow lines on the pent roof and the two sides of the gable. I also draw the narrow line beneath the frieze. This will require three drawings.

I measure the width of the first molding on the gables and draw a line halfway between the edge of the gable and this line. Then I draw a second line halfway between the edge of the gable and the line just drawn. Finally, I measure the width of the molding between the frieze and the architrave and draw this line.

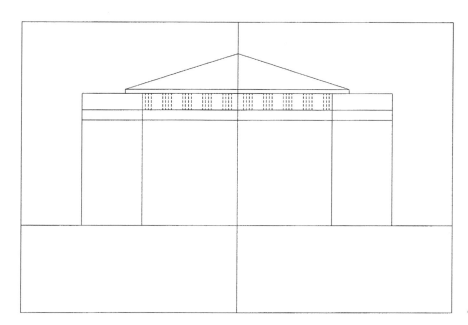

Step 4b. *The dentils are drawn.*

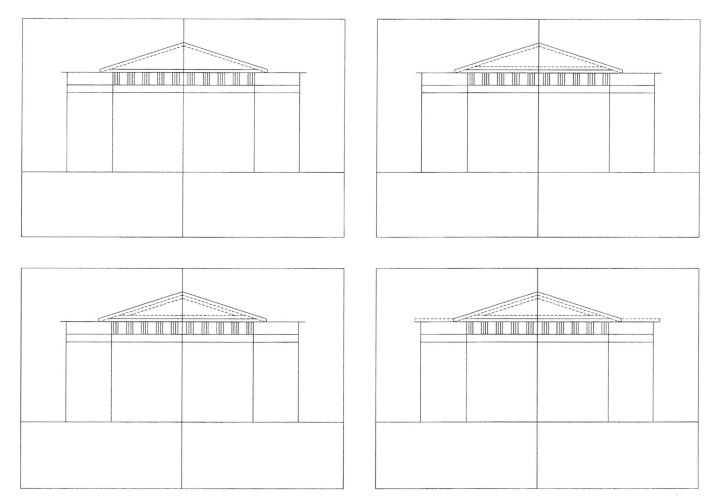

Step 5a. *The pediment is further defined.* Upper left, *the first line of molding on the gables is drawn.* Upper right, *the second line of molding on the pent roof is drawn.* Lower left, *the third line of molding on the gables is drawn.* Lower right, *the eaves on the main part of the building are drawn.*

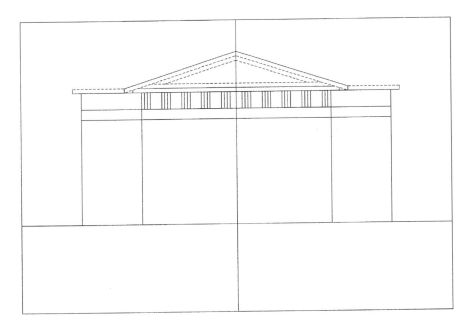

Step 5b. *The ends of the pent roof are defined by vertical lines.*

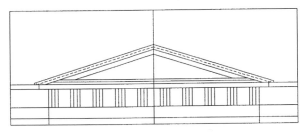
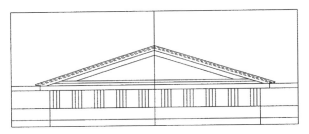

Step 6a. *The pediment and frieze are further refined.* Left, *a line halfway between the edge of the roof and the first molding on the gables is drawn.* Right, *a second line is drawn halfway between the edge of the gable and the previous line.*

Step 7. In this step I draw the two round windows on either side of the pediment and the lines for the roof over the wings of the main building. This requires five drawings.

First, I measure the space between the outer edges of the building and the end of the frieze, divide by four, and offset one line at that distance from the outer edge of the building and a second line the same distance from the outer edge of the colonnade. Next, I locate the center for each window by drawing the diameter of the windows, halfway between the eave and the top of the architrave. Then I measure and draw circles to represent the outer frame of each window. I draw a second circle inside each of these circles to represent the inner edge of the window frames. I measure the width of the mullions, divide by two, and draw the mullions, half on one side and the other half on the other side of the construction lines. I erase the construction lines.

Finally, I measure and draw the roof lines on the outer wings.

Step 8. In this step I define the location of the columns and the capitals on top of each column. This requires five drawings.

The columns of this building are Doric in design, the Doric being the oldest and simplest of the orders of Roman columns. The term "order" means a type of column having a particular *entablature*—that is, a particular capital and base. The capital of the Doric column consists of a narrow, square section directly beneath the architrave and a narrow, circular section with rounded edges between it and the top of the column. (Orders with more ornate entablature include the Ionic, the Tuscan, and the Corinthian.)

I measure the widths of the columns at their bases and draw vertical lines spacing the four columns beneath the

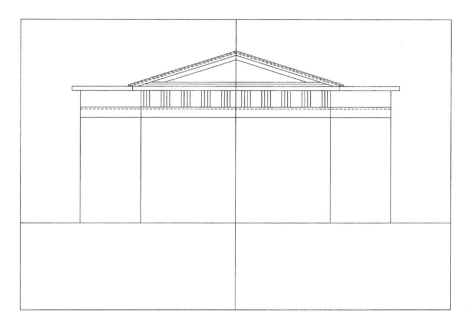

Step 6b. *The drawing of the pediment is completed with a narrow line beneath the frieze.*

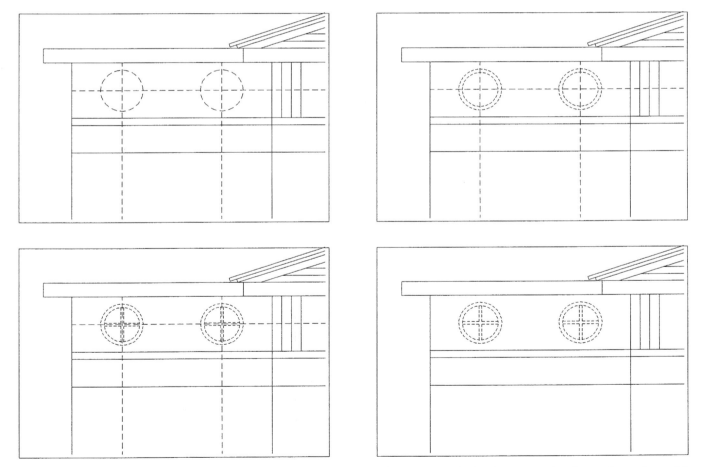

Step 7a. *The two round windows on either side of the pediment are drawn.* Upper left, *the center of each window is located by two vertical lines and a line halfway between the eaves and the top of the architrave.* Upper right, *two circles are drawn to represent the inner and outer edges of the window frames.* Lower left, *the mullions are drawn, half on one side and half on the other side of the construction lines.* Lower right, *the construction lines are erased.*

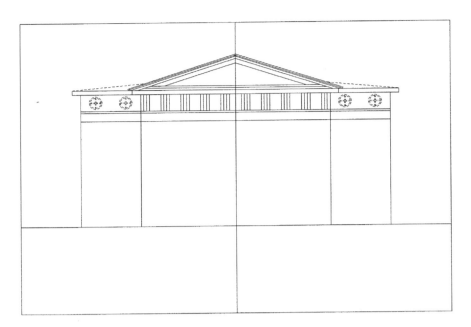

Step 7b. *The lines for the roof over the wings of the main building are drawn.*

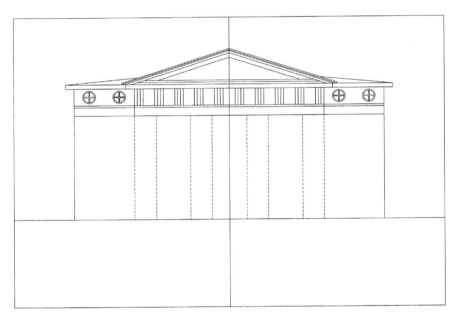

Step 8a. *The columns and the capitals atop each column are drawn. First, the widths of the columns at their bases are measured, and eight vertical lines are drawn spacing the four columns beneath the architrave.*

architrave. I measure the widths of the columns below the capitals and offset lines this distance from the outer measurement of each column.

I measure the width of the two parts of the capitals and draw horizontal lines representing them. I divide in half the two lines representing the bottom section of the capital. Then I erase the portions of these lines between the column. Next, I draw the radius at the ends of the bottom section of the capitals and draw arcs the same diame-

ter as the width of the bottom section of the capitals at each end, using the middle line as the center for these arcs. I erase the middle line and that portion of the inner column line that lies within the capitals.

I draw a line from the intersection of the inner line of each column with its capital to the intersection of the outer line with the base of the colonnade. Then, I erase both the inner and outer column construction lines. This leaves a column slightly tapering from top to bottom. In reality this

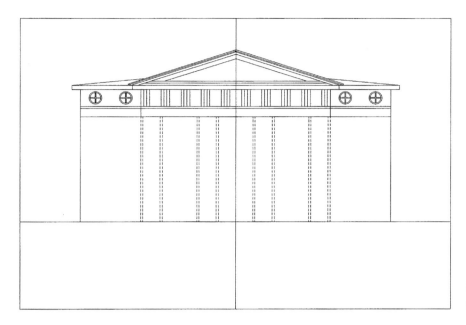

Step 8b. *Lines are drawn representing the width of each column just below the capital.*

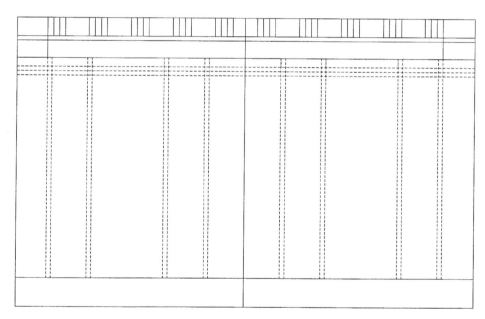

Step 8c. *Horizontal lines are drawn representing the width of the two parts of the capitals. The bottom section of the capital is divided into two equal sections.*

taper would have been in the form of a gentle curve called *entasis,* a sophisticated technique developed by Greek architects to make the edges of the columns appear as straight lines. Columns otherwise appear to curve inward, as a result of an optical illusion caused by the narrowing of the vertical lines.

Step 9. In this step I draw construction lines for the frames of the four windows.

I measure from the bottom of the photograph to the bottom edge of the windows and draw an offset this distance. I repeat for the inner edge of the bottom of the frame, the inner edge of the top of the frame, and the outer edge of the top of the frame. I measure in from the left side of the photograph and determine the outer and inner vertical edges of each window and offset these lines on the computer. However, I center each window within the space in which it is located.

Step 8d. *The lines between the columns are erased. Arcs the same diameter as the width of the bottom section of the capitals are drawn at each end, using the middle line as the center for these arcs.*

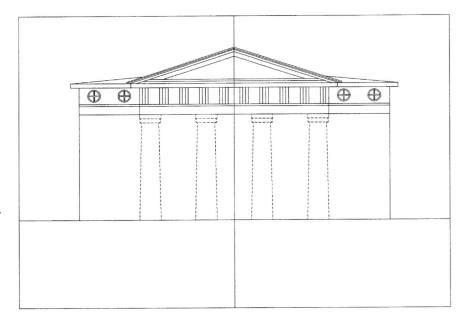

Step 8e. *The centerline is erased. A line is drawn from the intersection of the inner line of each column with its capital to the intersection of the outer line with the base of the colonnade, and the construction lines are erased. This leaves a column slightly tapering from top to bottom.*

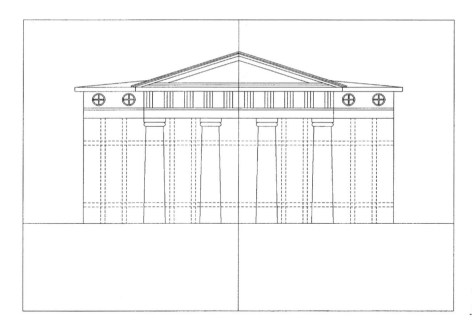

Step 9. *The construction lines for the frames of the four windows are drawn.*

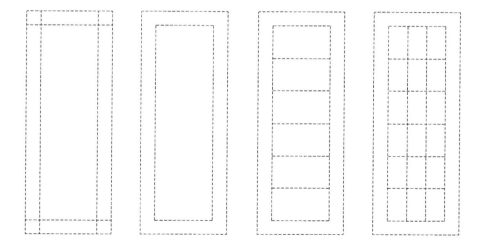

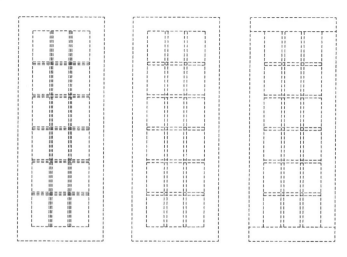

Step 10a. Far top left, *the construction lines outside the window frame are erased.* Center top left, *the construction lines between the inner and outer frame are erased.* Center top right, *each window is divided vertically into six spaces.* Far top right, *each window is divided horizontally into three spaces.* Far bottom left, *the mullions dividing each pane are drawn.* Center bottom left, *the construction lines are erased from inside the mullions.* Center bottom right, *the lintel and sill are extended to the outer edges of the frame.*

Step 10. In this step I draw the individual window-panes. This requires eight drawings.

I trim the lines extending from the edges of the window frames and those between the inner and outer edge of each frame. I measure and divide each window into six spaces vertically. Then I divide each window into three spaces horizontally. I measure the width of the mullions and draw the mullions dividing each pane. Finally, I erase the construction lines from inside the mullions. I repeat

the process for the remaining three windows. By using my CAD program's copy feature, I only have to draw one window and then can copy it as many times as I want at the desired locations.

Step 11. In this step I draw the door between the two central columns and the bases for each of the columns. In the photograph, the columns have no bases. However, in traditional Classical Revival architecture, the columns do.

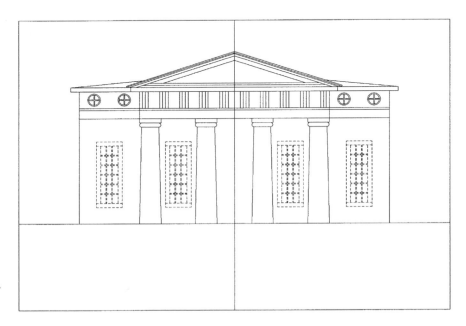

Step 10b. *The first window is copied at the other three locations.*

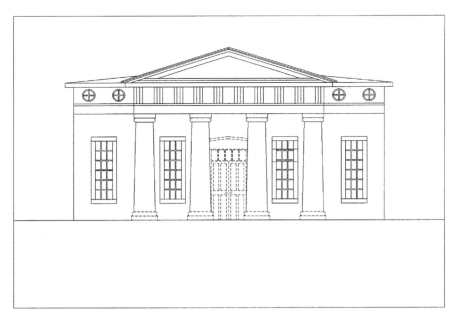

Step 11. *The door is drawn between the two central columns, following the same procedures used in drawing the windows. A traditional Classical Revival base is drawn at the bottom of each column, using the same procedures used for drawing the capitals.*

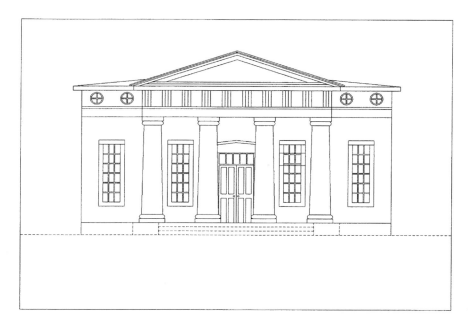

Step 12. *Three steps are drawn, and the bottom line of the bottom step is extended to the edges of the rectangle surrounding the building. The bottom edges of the rectangle are trimmed to complete the drawing.*

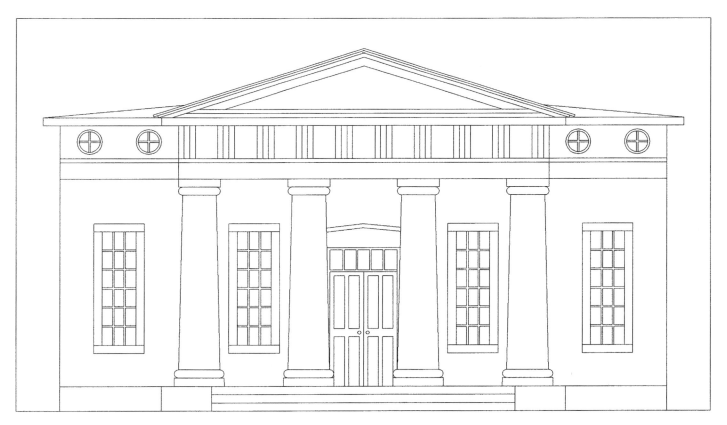

Step 13. *The building is scaled to its finished size.*

Because the bottom of the columns look unfinished in the photograph, I decided to add bases to them. I use the same procedures for drawing the door as those used in step 10 for drawing windows and the same procedures for the bases as those used in step 8 for drawing capitals, although reversing the square and circular sections.

Step 12. At this point I had planned to draw the fifteen steps leading up to the colonnade. However, I thought so many steps would look awkward in a miniature building and decided to use only three steps, extending the bottom line of the bottom step to the edges of the rectangle surrounding the building. I trimmed the bottom edges of the rectangle to complete the drawing.

Step 13. In this step I determine the finished size of the building.

As described in chapter 2, I measure the height of the door—.85 inches—and divide it into the optimum height for a door in a miniature building—1.5 inches. This gives me 1.76 (1.5 ÷ .85) or 176 percent. I then use the scale feature of my CAD program and enlarge the drawing by 176 percent. This results in a drawing of the bank that is 3.9 inches high and 6.69 inches long. I modify the area surrounding the building until the entire drawing measures 4.25 inches by 7.25 inches.

Now that the bank has been scaled to size, the drawing is ready to be copied and used to make a miniature.

22
END NOTES

Privy, outhouse, necessary, back house, loo, thunder box—no matter what it was called, the outside toilet was as necessary to rural America as barns, corncribs, and houses. The toilets didn't vary greatly in design except for the number of people they could accommodate at one time or for seats at different heights to accommodate both children and adults. Privies are still in use today, most still looking the same as they have for hundreds of years. During the Depression of the 1930s, the Federal Works Progress Administration created jobs constructing brick privies that used a composting system to manage the waste. They were known as "Roosevelt Monuments."

As simple as they were in architecture, outhouses needed both ventilation and light. Consequently, designs were cut into the doors to provide for both. At schools and other community buildings, symbols cut out of the door distinguished the privies by sex. For women it was the moon; for men it was the sun. Other symbols such as the German heart also were used, presumably for private homes where no gender differentiation was needed.

The Pennsylvania German constructing an outhouse made the symbol with nothing more complex than a compass for drawing the design and a keyhole saw to cut it out. The symbol of the sun was made with a large circle, the circumference of which was divided into eight sections. Each section was then formed into points using half-circles. The symbol for the moon was made using two circles the same size spaced a bit apart from one another. The German heart was made using six small circles touching one another.

I am not going to tell you how to color these privies. However, I used the coloring schemes from earlier buildings as guides—the Pennsylvania bank barn for the red one, the Fisher-Martin House for the weathered one, and the Kutztown Depot for the cream-colored one.

Three privies

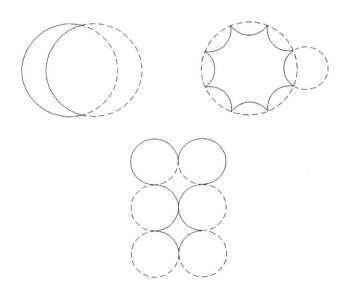

Pennsylvania German designs. *The broken lines in the designs indicate the portions of the circles that are erased. (Upper left) The moon design is drawn using two circles. (Upper right) The scalloped edge of the sun design is drawn using eight overlapping circles. Only one is shown. (Bottom center) The German heart is drawn using six circles that touch one another.*

With these buildings we come to the end of your adventure in making miniature wooden villages. If you made them all, your shelves must be full, so share them with friends and relatives. Who knows? They might ask for more, and before you know it you'll be in business.

For my part, I hope that not only have you found the book and making these buildings both informative and instructive, but also that you find yourself looking at the architecture in your community with a whole new insight.

LIST OF COLORED PENCILS

Both Berol Prismacolor and Derwent Artist colored pencils were used in the color rendering of the buildings in this book. I have added a suffix—PC or D—to differentiate between the two brands. There are no equiva-lent substitutes for the Derwent colored pencils. The Berol Prismacolor pencils are of American manufacture; the Derwent pencils are made in England.

BEROL PRISMACOLOR PENCILS
- apple green PC912
- aquamarine PC905
- black PC935
- blue slate PC1024
- blush pink PC928
- burnt ochre PC943
- carmine red PC926
- clay rose PC1017
- cloud blue PC1023
- cool gray 20% PC1060
- cool gray 50% PC1063
- cool gray 70% PC1065
- Copenhagen blue PC906
- cream PC914
- crimson red PC924
- dark brown PC946
- dark green PC908
- dark purple PC931
- dark umber PC947
- deco orange PC1010
- French gray 20% PC1069
- French gray 50% PC1072
- French gray 70% PC1074
- goldenrod PC1034
- grass green PC909
- imperial violet PC1007
- indigo blue PC901
- jade green PC1021
- light aqua PC992
- light cerulean blue PC904
- light peach PC927
- light umber PC941
- lilac PC956
- metallic copper PC951
- metallic green PC1048
- mulberry PC995
- olive green PC911
- orange PC918
- pale vermilion PC921
- parrot green PC1006
- peach PC939
- peacock blue PC1027
- periwinkle PC1025
- pink PC929
- poppy red PC922
- rosy beige PC1019
- sepia PC948
- sienna brown PC945
- terra cotta PC944
- Tuscan red PC937
- ultramarine PC902
- violet blue PC933
- warm gray 20% PC1051
- warm gray 50% PC1054
- warm gray 70% PC1056
- white PC938
- yellow ochre PC942
- yellowed orange PC1002

DERWENT STUDIO COLORED PENCILS
- blue gray D-68
- bottle green D-43
- cobalt blue D-31
- copper beech D-61
- dark violet D-25
- deep cadmium D-6
- deep vermilion D-14
- delft blue D-28
- geranium lake D-15
- imperial purple D-23
- indigo D-36
- light violet D-26
- madder carmine D-19
- raw sienna D-58
- rose madder lake D-21
- rose pink D-18
- sky blue D-34
- smalt blue D-30
- spectrum orange D-11
- straw yellow D-5
- water green D-44

METRIC CONVERSIONS

INCHES TO MILLIMETERS

in.	mm	in.	mm
1	25.4	51	1295.4
2	50.8	52	1320.8
3	76.2	53	1346.2
4	101.6	54	1371.6
5	127.0	55	1397.0
6	152.4	56	1422.4
7	177.8	57	1447.8
8	203.2	58	1473.2
9	228.6	59	1498.6
10	254.0	60	1524.0
11	279.4	61	1549.4
12	304.8	62	1574.8
13	330.2	63	1600.2
14	355.6	64	1625.6
15	381.0	65	1651.0
16	406.4	66	1676.4
17	431.8	67	1701.8
18	457.2	68	1727.2
19	482.6	69	1752.6
20	508.0	70	1778.0
21	533.4	71	1803.4
22	558.8	72	1828.8
23	584.2	73	1854.2
24	609.6	74	1879.6
25	635.0	75	1905.0
26	660.4	76	1930.4
27	685.8	77	1955.8
28	711.2	78	1981.2
29	736.6	79	2006.6
30	762.0	80	2032.0
31	787.4	81	2057.4
32	812.8	82	2082.8
33	838.2	83	2108.2
34	863.6	84	2133.6
35	889.0	85	2159.0
36	914.4	86	2184.4
37	939.8	87	2209.8
38	965.2	88	2235.2
39	990.6	89	2260.6
40	1016.0	90	2286.0
41	1041.4	91	2311.4
42	1066.8	92	2336.8
43	1092.2	93	2362.2
44	1117.6	94	2387.6
45	1143.0	95	2413.0
46	1168.4	96	2438.4
47	1193.8	97	2463.8
48	1219.2	98	2489.2
49	1244.6	99	2514.6
50	1270.0	100	2540.0

The above table is exact on the basis: 1 in. = 25.4 mm

U.S. TO METRIC

1 inch = 2.540 centimeters
1 foot = .305 meter
1 yard = .914 meter
1 mile = 1.609 kilometers

METRIC TO U.S.

1 millimeter = .039 inch
1 centimeter = .394 inch
1 meter = 3.281 feet or 1.094 yards
1 kilometer = .621 mile

INCH-METRIC EQUIVALENTS

Fraction	Decimal Equivalent Customary (in.)	Metric (mm)	Fraction	Decimal Equivalent Customary (in.)	Metric (mm)
$1/64$ — .015		0.3969	$33/64$ — .515		13.0969
$1/32$ — .031		0.7938	$17/32$ — .531		13.4938
$3/64$ — .046		1.1906	$35/64$ — .546		13.8906
$1/16$ — .062		1.5875	$9/16$ — .562		14.2875
$5/64$ — .078		1.9844	$37/64$ — .578		14.6844
$3/32$ — .093		2.3813	$19/32$ — .593		15.0813
$7/64$ — .109		2.7781	$39/64$ — .609		15.4781
$1/8$ — .125		3.1750	$5/8$ — .625		15.8750
$9/64$ — .140		3.5719	$41/64$ — .640		16.2719
$5/32$ — .156		3.9688	$21/32$ — .656		16.6688
$11/64$ — .171		4.3656	$43/64$ — .671		17.0656
$3/16$ — .187		4.7625	$11/16$ — .687		17.4625
$13/64$ — .203		5.1594	$45/64$ — .703		17.8594
$7/32$ — .218		5.5563	$23/32$ — .718		18.2563
$15/64$ — .234		5.9531	$47/64$ — .734		18.6531
$1/4$ — .250		6.3500	$3/4$ — .750		19.0500
$17/64$ — .265		6.7469	$49/64$ — .765		19.4469
$9/32$ — .281		7.1438	$25/32$ — .781		19.8438
$19/64$ — .296		7.5406	$51/64$ — .796		20.2406
$5/16$ — .312		7.9375	$13/16$ — .812		20.6375
$21/64$ — .328		8.3384	$53/64$ — .828		21.0344
$11/32$ — .343		8.7313	$27/32$ — .843		21.4313
$23/64$ — .359		9.1281	$55/64$ — .859		21.8281
$3/8$ — .375		9.5250	$7/8$ — .875		22.2250
$25/64$ — .390		9.9219	$57/64$ — .890		22.6219
$13/32$ — .406		10.3188	$29/32$ — .906		23.0188
$27/64$ — .421		10.7156	$59/64$ — .921		23.4156
$7/16$ — .437		11.1125	$15/16$ — .937		23.8125
$29/64$ — .453		11.5094	$61/64$ — .953		24.2094
$15/32$ — .468		11.9063	$31/32$ — .968		24.6063
$31/64$ — .484		12.3031	$63/64$ — .984		25.0031
$1/2$ — .500		12.7000	1 — 1.000		25.4000